TEXT MESSAGING

TEXT MESSAGING

A Conversation on Preaching

DOUGLAS D. WEBSTER

CLEMENTS PUBLISHING
Toronto

Clements Publishing
6021 Yonge Street, Box 213
Toronto, Ontario
M2M 3W2 Canada
www.clementspublishing.com

The author and publisher wish to thank Susan Montoya
for her creative work on the cover and Jim Meals
for his editorial assistance.

Library and Archives Canada Cataloguing in Publication

Webster, Douglas D.
Text messaging : a conversation on preaching /
Douglas D. Webster.

Includes bibliographical references.
ISBN 978-1-894667-96-8

1. Preaching. 2. Information technology—Religious
aspects—Christianity. 3. Communication—Religious aspects—
Christianity. 4. Text messages (Telephone systems). I. Title.

BV4211.3.W437 2010 251   C2009-906546-0

CONTENTS

For Virginia Webster

in gratitude for her wisdom and wit

INTRODUCTION

JESUS TALK

I want to explore the meaning of messaging the gospel text in our text messaging savvy culture. My purpose is not to knock technology. I'm all for Blackberries and iPhones. What I am concerned about is our trained incapacity to preach the gospel in this dot.com, hyper-linked world. I want to rediscover the priority of the Gospel Text. Instead of "dumbing down" the Gospel story and editing the Canon for what we find relevant, we ought to let *salvation history* and the *intensity of the text* shine through in all of its complexity and mystery. The truth of God revealed to us in the Bible and through salvation history deserves our careful attention. It is ironic that as our culture has become more sophisticated in its methods of communication it has insisted on a simplistic message. As the speed of communications has increased so has our apparent impatience with the message itself. But it is here that we have to resist the reduction of the Gospel to sound-bites and insist on comprehending the whole counsel of God. I can't help but believe that there are many people who long for a passionate, in-depth proclamation of God's story from Genesis to Revelation.

Our inability to think deeply about virtually anything has had a huge impact on preaching. Today's sermonizing takes this into account, whether intentionally or unintentionally, and seeks to compensate by trying to hold onto people's attention through humor, anecdotes, and bullet-point propositions. I recently attended a one day conference for pastors. I went expecting to be challenged and fed. I asked a pastor friend to go with me. Three hours of in-depth Bible teaching on our holy vocation and a good conversation over lunch was just what my soul needed. But instead, along with several hundred pastors, we were pedantically instructed in bullet-point, proof-text fashion on the basics, such as the meaning of "deacon" and how many times "baptism" is referred to in Acts.

I was dumbfounded. The speaker seemed to be gearing his presentation for a new member's class, and even then it seemed like he was dumbing down the gospel. But what amazed me even more was the response of the pastors. They were laughing at the speaker's jokes and dutifully taking down notes. They were perfectly content and having a good time. Meanwhile, I was thinking that a steady diet of this will leave us all spiritually anaesthetized. Is anyone else tired of listening to a pompous person delivering god-talk dribble that doesn't even come close to applying the Word of God to the situation we find ourselves in today? Preaching has become pragmatic and self-oriented. Its pragmatic goal is to communicate to the spiritual consumer little more than a "customized personal spiritual growth plan." And then we wonder why our congregations are spiritually illiterate. I am confident, however, that there are lay-people who are thinking more deeply about the Word of God than their pastors.

There is a growing inability of Christians to talk about their faith in Christ in any kind of meaningful way, especially outside the bounds of Sunday school, sermons and small group Bible studies. Sermons have largely become a recital of evangelical platitudes, privately prepared, without interaction with the thinking and praying community. They are publicly performed without lasting impact, usually in a style that does not flow from or serve the text. And these days it seems that most Christians are listening to sermons designed for someone else – the seeker or the young Christian. The preacher is complimented for execution, not for disciple-making. Thousands gather every Sunday to hear what they have heard many times before. There is a large and appreciative market of religious consumers who want to be given a recital of familiar truths. The impact of this kind of preaching leads to bigger auditoriums, filled with strangers who rarely fellowship beyond their familiar cliques. Consequently, it is becoming more difficult to distinguish between that which is done for spiritual growth and that which is done for public relations.

Christian communication has virtually no context outside of the pulpit. No one wants to hear from the pastor about these things over lunch or in casual conversation, and most pastors only want to talk about administrative matters, church politics, visionary programs and new trends. Any attempt to bring Jesus up in any kind of meaningful way outside the prescribed bounds feels like a violation of social etiquette. Gossip and small talk have largely replaced the Gospel in every arena but the pulpit, and even there the danger now exists for the sermon to be co-opted by mere sentiment and self-expression.

We talk freely about sports, food, fashions, stocks, celebrities, and politics, but serious talk about the Kingdom of God is almost nonexistent. We should not be surprised. Vast numbers of believers attend church in anonymity. One can go to church without ever uttering a word or making real eye contact. An awkward greeting time will not free us up to talk about following Jesus. On religious matters many are well schooled, but they show little signs of a meaningful relationship with God. They look bored in Sunday School and find it difficult to interact with a pedantic lesson that they have heard hundreds of times before. We have little capacity for meaningful dialogue on the very truths that we say we are so committed to on Sunday. We have unwittingly retreated from the Word without noting its absence. It has become "ossified with clichés, unexamined definitions, and leftover words."[1] Recovering the sacred text in a world of constant text messaging is our challenge. Let's retrace our steps and explore the origins of texting—Gospel style.

---

1.   George Steiner, *Language & Silence: Essays on Language, Literature, and the Inhuman* (New Haven, Conn: Yale University Press, 1998), p. 26.

1

TEXTING

The word *text* is an old Latin word with roots in the textile industry. It comes from the root word *tex-ere* to weave. *Texture* literally means the process or art of weaving. The idea of weaving a garment and weaving a story is linked linguistically and in the imagination. There is a connection between weaving strands of yarn together and weaving a narrative out of verbs, nouns, and adjectives. The story is to our soul what the shirt on our back is to our body. In the absence of textile and text, we are naked body and soul.

The word *text* in today's vernacular is linked to the technical process of conveying information. When we hear the phrase *text messaging,* we think of data processing: the speedy transmission of binary information over the Internet. This new form of communication replaces the slow art of weaving a narrative and telling a story. The relational power of speech and story is reduced to efficient sound bites of constant chatter. Communication has become a matter of connecting rather than communion.

My wife teaches remedial English at a community college. Her students are very proficient in text messaging in the technical sense. They have a one-handed blind mastery of the keyboard with the ability to surreptitiously text from their pockets while maintaining their typically bored expression. They may not be able to write a thesis statement and their vocabulary is limited, but they can text message with ease and efficiency. Most of my wife's students were never read to when they were children. Sharing family meals and reading a bedtime story were uncommon in their early childhood experience, but as young adults they possess the latest technology for texting their friends. In a generation, we have gone from letter writing to email to text messaging, and the nature of how and why we communicate has changed.

My thesis is that we are working with two forms of text messaging: one original and the other modern. The ancient form is storied communication; the contemporary form is data transmission. The tension is between narrativity and networking: stories that transform us in the world and systems that conform us to the world. The original use of the word *text* has an even more singular meaning than weaving just any story. In Medieval Latin *Textus* referred specially to the one story that redeems all of our individual stories. *Textus* was another name for the Gospel—the Christian meta-narrative. Students of Koine Greek are familiar with the term *Textus Receptus,* the name given to the earliest extant manuscripts for the Greek New Testament. For Christians, the text is the Bible and text messaging is the art of weaving the story of the Gospel into the subtext of our lives. Preaching aims to do that by paying close attention to the salvation story and telling the story with insight and intensity.

Technical text messaging is made possible by space communication satellites and digital technology, which grew out of the need for technicians to efficiently transmit data among themselves. Today SMS (Short Message System) is a global multibillion dollar growth industry used by millions of people to send cryptic instant messages, an endless stream of miscellaneous Babel speech in dot.com-hyper-drive.

Revelational text messaging is grounded in the Word that was made flesh and dwelt among us.[1] God chose language as the primary medium to communicate his salvation to us. The Word captures the essence of the Incarnation of God. God "embodied in the neighborhood" reveals the message of God full of grace and truth. As a corollary to this truth, the Holy Scriptures are described as God-breathed and necessary for essential instruction "so that all God's people may be thoroughly equipped for every good work." These two types of text messaging, technical and revelational, train us in two very different forms of communication. We want to explore these differences and understand the implications for preaching.

NETWORKING VS. NARRATIVITY

Skip over the negative uses of text messaging such as sexting, cheating, addicting, distracting, and trivializing, and few would disagree that text messaging is a useful and efficient tool for staying connected. But it would be a stretch to argue that texting builds community. For that, we need something more than a Blackberry or an iPhone. We need to become part of the story, not just any story, but God's story. To acquire this narrativity—this storied community, we need to immerse ourselves

---

1. John 1:14

in salvation history. The difference between these two forms of text messaging is as great as the physical disparity between "Blackberry thumb" and Baptism. The former describes the orthopedic malady of incessant text messaging – a sore thumb; the latter describes total immersion in the story of Jesus Christ—baptized into his death and raised into his life. Against the fast-paced Internet chatter that coincides with our helter-skelter frenetic existence, we need to sit quietly and immerse ourselves in the biblical text. As we will see, there are a number of reasons that make reading, meditating, praying and contemplating a biblical text difficult for us to do.

Perhaps it was never easy. But in this age awash with Christian resources at our fingertips, designed for easy accessibility and a fourth grade reading level, we have nearly hit the wall when it comes to hearing God's Word. The canon for most Christian young people is not the Canon of Scripture but Hollywood's cinematic blockbusters. Pastors lament biblical illiteracy and Christian publishers justify their popular bestsellers as what the market wants. In an age of information overload there is "a famine of hearing the words of the Lord."[2]

A trained incapacity to think and communicate on anything other than the shallow level of small talk, sound-bite snippets, and instant messaging has been acquired over time. We have retreated from the Word by choosing numbers over thought, scanning over reading, and images over words. Ironically, we have chosen this for ourselves. Text messaging is symptomatic of the famine in the land—a famine for meaningful dialogue and the Word of God.

---

2. Amos 8:11.

One of the world's leading literary critics, professor George Steiner describes the retreat from the word in history, sociology, philosophy, ethics, and even in aesthetic choice and music. Everything today is by the numbers. Statistics, polls, and a calculable theoretic basis, are the new oracles in today's world. Steiner writes, "The most decisive change in the tenor of Western intellectual life since the 17th century is the submission of successively larger areas of knowledge to the modes and proceedings of mathematics . . . "[3] The meaning we value as a culture can be reduced to data processing. "Large areas of meaning and praxis now belong to such nonverbal languages as mathematics, symbolic logic, and formulas of chemical or electronic relation."[4] Steiner argues that we have many more English words today than we did in Shakespeare's day. Modern English has some 600,000 words compared to Elizabethan English's 150,000. "Shakespeare's working vocabulary exceeds that of any later author, and the King James Bible, although it requires only 6000 words, suggests that the conception of literacy prevailing at the time was far more comprehensive than ours. The real point lies not in the number of words potentially available, but in the degree to which the resources of language are in actual current use."[5]

In the late 1950s, Steiner observed that "music is today the central fact of lay culture," adding, somewhat quaintly, "Many gather before the hi-fi set or join in musical performance."[6] Obviously, he did not envision the ubiquitous iPod, but he understood the impact that this retreat from the word would

---

3.   Steiner, p. 15.
4.   Steiner, p. 24.
5.   Steiner p. 25.
6.   Steiner, p. 30.

have on thinking and communications. "The tempo of urban and industrial life leaves one exhausted at nightfall. When one is tired, music, even difficult music, is easier to enjoy than serous literature . . . In short, the musical sound, and to a lesser degree the work of art and its reproduction, are beginning to hold a place in literate society once firmly held by the word."[7] Steiner feared that growing specialization (with each field of study having its own language) would lead to "mutual incomprehension" and the breakdown of communication. He wrote, "Everywhere, knowledge is splintering into intense specialization, guarded by technical languages fewer and fewer of which can be mastered by an individual mind. Our awareness of the complication of reality is such that those unifications or syntheses of understanding which made common speech possible no longer work. Or they work only at the rudimentary level of daily need."[8] Steiner was aware that the towers of babel were proliferating, making networking essential and narrativity nearly impossible.

Nicholas Carr asks, "Is Google Making Us Stupid?" in his article by that title in *The Atlantic*. His thesis is this: "Our capacity for reflection and understanding has retracted, as our ability to sort through the data has expanded." Online searching, surfing and scanning are changing the way we think. Carr explains,

> Over the past few years I've had an uncomfortable sense that someone, or something, has been tinkering with my brain, remapping the neural circuitry, reprogramming the memory. My mind isn't going—so far as I can tell—but it's changing. I'm not thinking the way I used to think. I can feel it most strongly

---

7.   Steiner, p. 30.
8.   Steiner, p. 34.

when I'm reading. Immersing myself in a book or a lengthy article used to be easy. My mind would get caught up in the narrative or the turns of the argument, and I'd spend hours strolling through long stretches of prose. That's rarely the case anymore. Now my concentration often starts to drift after two or three pages. I get fidgety, lose the thread, begin looking for something else to do. I feel as if I'm always dragging my wayward brain back to the text. The deep reading that used to come naturally has become a struggle. . . .What the Net seems to be doing is chipping away my capacity for concentration and contemplation. My mind now expects to take in information the way the Net distributes it: in a swiftly moving stream of particles. Once I was a scuba diver in the sea of words. Now I zip along the surface like a guy on a Jet Ski.[9]

Recently published studies on how people use the Net for research confirm that scanning, skimming, and hopping from one source to another is changing not only the way we read but the way we think. Our capacity for deep reading and reflection is weakening. "We are not only *what* we read," says Maryanne Wolf, a developmental psychologist at Tufts University. "We are *how* we read." Reading online tends to make readers "mere decoders of information." Carr writes, "Our ability to interpret text, to make the rich mental connections that form when we read deeply and without distraction, remains largely disengaged."

Carr describes Google's headquarters, in Mountain View, California, known as the Googleplex, as the Internet's high church, and insists that there is a distinctive philosophy of life emanating from this modern shrine. Google believes, according to Carr,

---

9. Nicholas Carr, "Is Google Making Us Stupid?" The Atlantic, July/August 2008, (http://www.theatlantic.com/doc/print/200807/google).

that intelligence is the output of a mechanical process, a series of discrete steps that can be isolated, measured, and optimized. In Google's world, the world we enter when we go online, there's little place for the fuzziness of contemplation. . . . The idea that our minds should operate as high-speed data-processing machines is not only built into the workings of the Internet, it is the network's reigning business model as well. The faster we surf across the Web—the more links we click and pages we view—the more opportunities Google and other companies gain to collect information about us and to feed us advertisements. Most of the proprietors of the commercial Internet have a financial stake in collecting the crumbs of data we leave behind as we flit from link to link—the more crumbs, the better. The last thing these companies want is to encourage leisurely reading or slow, concentrated thought. It's in their economic interest to drive us to distraction.

Quoting playwright Richard Foreman, Carr worries that we risk turning into "'pancake people'—spread wide and thin as we connect with that vast network of information accessed by the mere touch of a button."

Sociologist Robert Wuthnow studies the impact that this new style of thinking is having on the emerging adult generation.[10] Wuthnow calls this generation in their 20s and 30s a generation of tinkerers. They put life together "by improvising, by piecing together an idea from here, a skill from there, and a contact from somewhere else." They have a "do-it-yourself" mentality, as they cobble together a customized lifestyle. Wuthnow likens younger adults to "the farmer rummaging through the junk pile for makeshift parts. The spiritual tinkerer is able to shift through a veritable scrap heap of ideas and practices from

---

10.   Robert Wuthnow, *After the Baby Boomers: How Twenty-and Thirty-Somethings Are Shaping The Future of American Religion* (Princeton, NJ: Princeton University Press, 2007), p. 14.

childhood, from religious organizations, classes, conversations with friends, books, magazines, television programs, and Web sites. The tinkerer is free to engage in this kind of rummaging . . . Each individual claims the authority—in fact, the duty to make up his or her mind about what to believe."[11] Today's student tends to believe that there are no best answers, no one way to see things, no meta-narratives that orient all of life. They are their own best authority. They see themselves as in charge of cobbling together a worldview that works in a pluralistic culture. They have been trained "to hedge religious convictions in a language of opinion and feeling."[12]

The Oscar winning movie *Slum Dog Millionaire* illustrates the new epistemology of people in their twenties. Jamal Malik is a street kid (or "slumdog") who has landed an appearance on India's version of the hit TV game show *Who Wants to be a Millionaire?* Jamal exceeds expectations on the show, and the producers alert the police after they become suspicious of his methods. The young contestant is subsequently arrested and is interrogated by the police. As the interrogation proceeds, Jamal's story is told through harrowing flashbacks that show the terrible poverty of Mumbai and help explain how he knew the answers to the *Millionaire* questions. Everything he knows comes out of his personal experience. He has no formal education, but as fate would have it, the miscellaneous and haphazard collection of information that he has acquired along life's perilous journey is just what he needs to answer the random questions on the game show.

---

11. Wuthnow, p. 15.
12. Wuthnow, p. 121.

Book knowledge provides nothing useful for Jamal. He could be Wuthnow's global poster boy for his theory of tinkering. Life is a pluralistic junk yard with thoughts, ideologies, and random facts lying around. In the moment, Jamal seems to gather these up, because who knows when they may be useful. He cobbles together a worldview out of street savvy survival skills and his relational drive to be reunited with his childhood sweetheart and his brother. All of his knowledge is based on personal experience. The world of teaming masses, abject poverty, drug lords, and game show hype swirls around him. Jamal only appears to be dull, his blank demeanor serves as a cover. He is careful to give nothing away. He really is as wise as a serpent and as harmless as a dove. He illustrates the new epistemology: it is not what you are taught or what you study that counts. It is your ability to adapt to an ever-changing, life-threatening world, and knowing what you need to know to survive the evil and take advantage of a few lucky-breaks along the way.

Images over words favor networking over narrativity. Neil Postman in *Amusing Ourselves to Death: Public Discourse in the Age of Show Business*, defined exposition as the "sophisticated ability to think conceptually, deductively and sequentially," accompanied by "a high valuation of reason and order; an abhorrence of contradiction; a large capacity for detachment and objectivity; and a tolerance for delayed response."[13] His thesis was that toward the end of the 19th century we moved from the Age of Exposition to the Age of Show Business. We became accustomed to "an abundance of irrelevant information" thus altering what can be called the "information-action"

---

13. Neil Postman, *Amusing Ourselves to Death: Public Discourse in the Age of Show Business* (New York: Penguin, 1985), p. 63.

ratio. The cultural shift from words to images shrunk our attention span and decreased our capacity to weigh ideas, to compare and contrast assertions, to connect one generalization to another, to understand what moves us.[14] Postman argued that "television's way of knowing is uncompromisingly hostile to typography's way of knowing; that television's conversations promote incoherence and triviality; that the phrase 'serious television' is a contradiction in terms; and that television speaks in only one persistent voice—the voice of entertainment . . . Television is transforming our culture into one vast arena for show business."[15] Serious and thoughtful discourse is up against a barrage of images coming at us in ever increasing rapid succession. The news in depth is limited to a three minute segment. We have grown impatient with anything that requires critical thinking. According to Postman, television's anti-word philosophy of education is based on three commandments:

(1) Thou shalt have no prerequisites. TV does away with the idea that sequence and continuity have anything to do with thought. Immediate accessibility is demanded.

(2) Thou shalt induce no perplexity. Nothing has to be "remembered, studied, applied or, worst of all, endured." Contentment, not growth, is the aim.

(3) Thou shalt avoid exposition. "Arguments, hypotheses, discussions, reasons, refutations or any of the traditional instruments of reasoned discourse" are eliminated. Increase visual stimulation and reduce exposition.[16]

---

14. Postman, pp. 51, 54.
15. Postman, p.80.
16. Postman, pp. 147-148.

The impact of retreating from the word, scanning over reading, cobbling together a customized worldview, and preferring images to words, has not only changed the way we communicate, but the way we think. A generation ago the concern was to cultivate a Christ-centered worldview, now the challenge is to simply think about the gospel in any kind of meaningful way.

2

TEXTUS RECEPTUS

The motto of the Reformation was *Fides ex auditu*, drawing on the apostle Paul's declaration that, "Faith comes from hearing the message, and the message is heard through the Word of Christ."[1] Paul says this just after quoting from the prophet Isaiah, "Lord, who has believed our message?" and just before quoting from Psalm 19, "Their voice has gone out into all the earth, their words to the ends of the world." There is no doubt that the message has been communicated, but whether it has been truly heard is another matter. "The biblical exaltation of hearing over seeing is no happenstance," writes Ralph Wood. "The eye is often limited to surfaces, while the ear can penetrate depths . . . 'Obedience' derives, tellingly, from the Latin *audire*, 'to listen.' And since disobedience entails a refusal of the One who can be denied only through a kind of willed irrationality, the word 'absurdity' also has an aural etymology: surdus is Latin for 'deaf.' Jesus does not declare, therefore, 'Whoever has eyes to see, let him see,' but rather 'Whoever has

---

1.   Romans 10:17.

ears let them hear.'"[2]

When I think of "hearing," my grandad Webster comes to mind. He was hard-of-hearing, the result of working for years at the Bethlehem Steel Plant in Buffalo, New York. The daily assault on his ears of deafening industrial sounds rendered the normal human voice almost inaudible. I remember how hard it was to communicate with him. When we spoke to grandad, we had to shout and we had to think before we shouted so as to use as few words as possible. Some sounds, like the piercing whistle of a tea kettle he didn't hear at all, even with his hearing aid in. Since he was hard-of-hearing, he often withdrew from conversations and went off to smoke his pipe and sit by himself. Of course, whenever we said something in his presence that wasn't exactly meant for his ears, he heard it loud and clear! The family of God seems to have plenty of hard-of-hearing family members, like my grandfather, who easily disengage. They have grown used to being "out of it." They don't know what they're missing and they don't really care.

A pastor friend, Nate Landis, was born with one good ear and one ear that lacked any hearing apparatus. Consequently, Nate has to be very intentional about hearing. In a meeting he positions himself so he can hear out of his one good ear. Instead of concealing his disability, he deals with it openly, in a mature, mater-of-fact way. Nate is a great reminder to me of doing what it takes to hear the Word of God.

Textus Receptus is Latin for "received text" and refers to the Greek manuscripts Erasmus used to compose and publish his Greek New Testament. Erasmus' text was the primary source

---

2. Ralph Wood, *Flannery O'Connor and the Christ-Haunted South* (Grand Rapids, MI: Eerdmans, 2005), p. 161.

for Luther's translation of the Bible into German and William Tyndale's into English. Earlier manuscripts of the New Testament have been discovered since Erasmus' day and today's translations are based on these more reliable texts. The process of translating the Bible into people's mother tongue is ongoing, but the real struggle for many today is not reading the Bible in the vernacular but reading the Bible with understanding. The Reformers never could have imagined the array of Bibles we have to choose from, nor the level of biblical illiteracy afflicting the Western church so rich in resources. Most Christians have multiple Bibles in a variety of versions. On any given Sunday parishioners may be holding any one of a number of versions: KJV, RSV, NASB, NIV, TNIV, ESV, the Living Bible, or the Message. But the big question is this: Do we have ears to hear?

Eat this Book is Eugene Peterson's challenge to let the Bible metabolize in our lives. "Not merely *Read* your Bible but *Eat this Book*. Christians feed on Scripture. Holy Scripture nurtures the holy community as food nurtures the human body. Christians don't simply learn or study or use Scripture: we assimilate it, take it into our lives in such a way that it gets metabolized into acts of love, cups of cold water, missions into all the world, healing and evangelism and justice in Jesus' name, hands raised in adoration of the Father, feet washed in company with the Son."[3] Peterson begins with a parable describing his seven-year-old grandson Hans who has been given a New Testament. He doesn't know how to read, but he knows how adults look when they are reading. He opens up the book, holds it before his eyes, which move along the page just as if he was understanding

---

3. Eugene H. Peterson, *Eat This Book* (Grand Rapids, MI: Eerdmans, 2006), p. 18.

the words on the page. He looks like he's taking it all in. Hans knows he can't read. He's not faking it. Hans is honest. He freely admits, "I can't read" but he enjoys the act of reading—what it looks like to read and understand. Hans' "reading" is a parable of the church not hearing the Word of God. Luther declared the eyes to be hard of hearing and he urged his hearers to stick them in their ears when the Word of God is proclaimed.[4]

A DAVID PSALM

Psalm 40 is a psalm about hearing—the need to be heard and the need to hear. The psalm begins with God hearing the cry of the psalmist and rescuing him from the miry pit and the roaring flood. The result of being heard is God-given strength and security and the ability to sing a new song, "a hymn of praise to our God." We cry out to God in desperation and end up singing a praise song.

At the center of the psalm is the psalmist's deep felt need to hear God. Conventional thinking and ritual get in the way of this hearing. "Sacrifice and offering you did not desire—but my ears you have opened —burnt offerings and sin offerings you did not require." Literally the line goes, "You dug ears for me." Eugene Peterson writes, "Imagine a human head with no ears. A blockhead. Eyes, nose, and mouth, but no ears. Where ears are usually found there is only a smooth, impenetrable surface, granite bone. God speaks. No response. The metaphor occurs in the context of a bustling religious activity deaf to the voice of God . . . Hebrew sacrificial ritual included reading from a book, but the reading had degenerated into something done

---

4.   Wood, p. 163.

and watched."[5] Anyone can go through the liturgical motions without testimony and witness. Only after God has opened our ears are we ready for mission and proclamation. The implication is that we get stuck in our religious routines. It doesn't help to get the liturgy down pat and put our mind and heart in neutral. We need Yahweh to open up our hearing so we agree to do what Yahweh wants in place of burnt offerings.[6] It has always been about the worship life, not the worship service.

To hear God speak is vital for worship. Only then can we say, "Here I am, I have come—it is written about me in the scroll. I desire to do your will, my God; your law is within my heart."[7] Whoever has ears to hear understands the Word. Listening is the prerequisite for witness. "Instead of sealing our lips, hiding our thoughts and concealing God's love, we proclaim. We speak of God's faithfulness. The book is discovered to have a voice . . . The words invade the heart . . . The act of reading becomes an act of listening . . . The ear takes over from the eye and involves the heart."[8]

The psalmist is honest about the spiraling intensity of crying out to God, hearing the voice of God in his Word, and then proclaiming the salvation, justice and faithfulness in the great assembly. Life doesn't get any easier, because God listens to us and we listen to God. Listening to God may be disappointing. A ticket to success it is not, but it is the one sure way of knowing that we are known by the Lord. In communion and commu-

---

5. Eugene Peterson, *Working the Angles* (Grand Rapids, MI: Eerdmans, 1987), p. 70.

6. John Goldingay, *Psalms*, vol 1. (Grand Rapids, MI: Baker, 2006), p. 573.

7. Psalm 40:6-8.

8. Peterson, *Working the Angles*, pp. 70-71.

nication there is a spiraling cycle of intensity: the worshiper cries out / sings / hears / proclaims, which corresponds to God hearing and delivering. As life intensifies, our need and relationship with God remain constant. Pain and Praise go hand-in-hand. *Instead of treating the Bible like a collection of sayings to be read like fortune cookies broken open at random, we enter into the world of the text through meditation.* Through prayer we enter into an unforced conversation with God. His Word is inviting, commanding, challenging, rebuking, judging, comforting, and directing, but not imposing, manipulative, coercive, and oppressive. Through contemplation we engage the Word in the moment-by-moment activities, chores, routines, duties, and pleasures of daily life. The contemplative life is not lived in isolation but in immersion.[9]

Christi Napier has cried out to God, listened to God and proclaimed the truth of God. This young wife and mother of two has undergone twenty-six surgeries on her throat and esophagus over the last two years. Christi embraced her calling and accepted her ministry of suffering and weakness, but it hasn't been easy. A year ago she was driving home from a Bible study, when she broke down and cried out to the Lord, "I just need this to end." In that desperate moment, Christi recalls that the Lord spoke into her heart and said, "You don't need this to end. You just need me." Upon hearing that inaudible word from the Lord, Christi felt a wonderful wave of freedom break over her and she realized that she didn't ever need to panic. In response, Christi's witness is strong, "I don't need certain circumstances to have the peace and rest and loving service in the Lord that I so deeply desire. I just need God."

9. Peterson, *Eat This Book,* pp. 99, 101, 109.

A JESUS PARABLE

The parable of the sower and the soils is a parable about hearing.[10] The imagery of the seed reminds us of Isaiah's references to the holy seed, the tender shoot, and the Root of Jesse. Jesus issued a coded message when he said, "A farmer went out to sow his seed . . . " The parable was designed to perk up ears to what the prophet Isaiah said about bad fruit and barren vineyards.[11] We were meant to recall the promise of the holy seed and abundant fruit.[12] *These metaphors were not meant to be interpreted with technical precision but with poetic fusion.* Jesus identified the seed as the Word of God and implied that he was the Sower. With Isaiah's metaphors of the holy seed and the tender shoot in mind, it is not difficult for us to merge the metaphors of seed and sower into one. In Jesus, the Living Word, we have the fulfillment of Isaiah's prophecy. "A shoot will come up from the stump of Jesse; from his roots a Branch will bear fruit. The Spirit of the Lord will rest on him—the Spirit of wisdom and of understanding, the Spirit of counsel and of power, the Spirit of knowledge and of the fear of the Lord."[13]

The parable resonates with Isaiah's prophecies of blessing and salvation. The "holy seed" is taking root, but instead of celebrating, the parable cautions the hearer. Scattering the seed is a blessing, but the destruction of the seed is a sober warning. From a secular point of view Jesus was at the height of his career when he gave this parable about hearing. Wherever he went, he attracted large crowds. Yet the parable is mainly about

---

10.   Luke 8:1-15
11.   Isaiah 5
12.   Isaiah 27
13.   Isaiah 11:1-2

rejection. Jesus points out "how frequently the divine seed is destroyed—destroyed in stony hearts, by the heat of the sun, by choking thorns and predatory birds—this is why there is in this parable a deep sense of grief and sorrow." The meaning of the parable prompted Helmut Thielicke to ask, "I wonder whether we have caught the sadness that hangs over this story?"[14]

Many people were in the audience, but they didn't have ears to hear. The crowds didn't get it. And Jesus reserved the interpretation of the story for the disciples' ears only. Matthew tells us that the disciples not only wanted to know the meaning of the parable, but they wanted to know why Jesus spoke to the people in parables. Jesus said, "The knowledge of the secrets of the kingdom of God has been given to you, but to others I speak in parables, so that, 'though seeing, they may not see; though hearing, they may not understand.'"[15]

The parable called for reflection and invited questions, but the crowd was apparently content to leave without understanding the meaning of the parable. Jesus identified with the prophet's call to ministry. Remember that Isaiah was such a straight-talking prophet that he drove people away from the truth. Isaiah presented the truth with such clarity, simplicity, effectiveness and sincerity, that each successive refusal to respond to the grace of God made it that much more difficult to hear the message. Isaiah was criticized for making his message too simple, "Who is he trying to teach?" asked his critics, "children!?"[16] Like Isaiah's audience, the crowds were

---

14. Helmut Thielicke, *The Waiting Father* (New York: Harper, 1959), p. 52.

15. Matthew 13:11-13; Isaiah 6:9.

16. Isaiah 28:9-10.

not responding to the message, but it wasn't Jesus' fault. They weren't listening!

No matter how loud and clear the message of the Kingdom of God came through in Jesus' proclamation many didn't have "eyes to see and ears to hear." The parable of the soils explains why. Jesus laid out the plain meaning of the parable. The "seed" represents the Word of God, the Gospel, the good news of Jesus. The "soil" represents the heart of the hearer and hearing is a metaphor for saving faith. Having faith and bearing fruit are one in the same.[17] A faithful, fruitful response to the Word of God is the product of a process of growth and development. We were meant to hear the Word, retain it and persevere in it. Nevertheless, in three out of the four "soil" types the goal of sowing the seed is not realized. In effect, Jesus warns, "Be careful to truly hear the Word of God, for some are hostile and reject it outright, others are enthusiastic at first, but quickly forget it when things don't go well, and still others are very conflicted about the Word of God and don't apply it consistently and personally."

Jesus illustrated people's inability to receive the Word of God in three ways. Seeds that fall on the beaten path don't have a chance to germinate and take root. The hard ground is an analogy for the hard hearted who are unable to really hear the good news of the Kingdom of God. This situation describes the person who has been robbed of the Word of God by the power of the evil one. They hear the Word, but then "the devil comes and takes away the word from their hearts, so that they cannot believe and be saved."[18] Jesus began by acknowledging

---

17. see John 15:1-6
18. Luke 8:12

the power of the evil one to prevent people from receiving the Word. This is not an excuse, but a statement of fact. Jesus never underestimated the power of evil. There are many ways the devil seeks to destroy the Gospel in people's lives. How difficult it must be for an abused child to believe in the love of God and a spoiled, materialist child may not fare any better. The devil uses many things to harden our hearts: money, sex, and power, to name three. But we should never say that it is impossible for anyone, including ourselves, to hear the Gospel, because we know that the Word of God "is as sharp as a surgeon's scalpel, cutting through everything, whether doubt or defense, laying us open to listen and obey." We agree with the writer of Hebrews, "Nothing and no one is impervious to God's Word."[19] Nevertheless, Jesus wanted his disciples to be aware of why some people don't respond. The devil has a hand in it. The seed of the Gospel never gets a chance to grow because evil snatches it away.

The second soil type is rocky. The seed falls to the ground and begins to grow, but its roots don't go down very deep. Jesus illustrated people who receive the Word with joy, "but in the time of testing they fall away." Such people may be drawn to the Gospel enthusiastically. They are thrilled and uplifted with the good news. They may feel inspired and "pumped" with their new found faith. They are like the people who "ate the loaves and had [their] fill," and wanted to make Jesus King.[20] They are waving palms and shouting Hosanna on Palm Sunday, but they're long gone on Good Friday. This shallow enthusiasm is a bigger problem than we may realize. We must not cater to it

---

19. Hebrews 4:12-12, The Message.
20. John 6:15, 26.

and turn a worshiping congregation into an audience hooked on entry-level preaching instead of the "whole counsel of God." J. I. Packer has characterized North American Protestantism as man-centered, manipulative, success-oriented, self-indulgent and sentimental. It is 3,000 miles wide and half an inch deep.[21] But what do we expect when we advertise conversion as "flipping a switch" instead explaining the cost of discipleship? There is a difference between feeling swept up in an emotional moment and taking up our cross and following Jesus. Is it any wonder that when the time of testing comes people move on to something else that will bring a feeling of excitement? This second soil type is not an excuse for us to change the way we present the Gospel. It is a warning to us that if we present the Word of God the way Jesus did this is what will happen. "For many are invited, but few are chosen."[22]

In the third illustration the seed falls among thorns. This represents those who hear the Word and begin to grow in Christ, but their growth is impaired by competition with other concerns, ambitions and passions. "They are choked by life's worries, riches and pleasures, and they do not mature." We know all too well how anxiety, money and self-indulgence impact the believer's maturity. In fact Jesus elaborated on each one of these problem areas with individual parables. But his emphasis here is on people's inability to grow spiritually and produce fruit. Worry, wealth, and worldliness can render us deaf to the Word of God. We may have become so steeped in

---

21. James I. Packer, *Quest for Godliness* (Wheaton, IL: Crossway, 1990), p. 22.

22. Matthew 22:14

the ethos of the culture that the Word no longer challenges our sinful ways.

I referred to my grandfather's hard-of-hearing condition earlier. After thirty years of exposure to the high decimal noise of a steel foundry we had to shout to get his attention. What happened to my grandfather's hearing, can happen to our hearing of the Word of God. How does thirty years in business impact an executive's hearing of the Word of God? How does four years of High School help or hurt a teenager's sensitivity to the will of God? How does suburbia change the way we hear the Word? Over-exposure to the "sounds" of our world may make us deaf to the specific truths of God's Word. Having been bombarded by the wisdom of the world, we don't even know what we are missing.

The first two soil conditions illustrate people's rejection of the Gospel, but the third type illustrates people's frustration with the Gospel. Instead of refusing to believe or falling away from faith in Christ, such people never mature in the faith. More often than not they stay in the church and blame others for their conflicted feelings and frustrations. Jesus' parable of the sower helps us understand why people don't receive the Word of God very well. It is sad that Jesus should have to explain to his disciples why people are not responding to the Gospel, but his explanation helps us to see what is happening in our own day. Our theology of communication is closely tied to our theology of church growth. Jesus didn't lift the weight of decision making and personal responsibility from people's shoulders. He stressed personal accountability. He communicated the Gospel clearly, but people had to respond faithfully. He neither manipulated nor modified the message to make it more popular. Jesus teaches us the difference between pleasing people and loving people. We "must love and understand people, but [we] must know and love still more the will and word of God"[23] What must die in everyone who seeks to communicate the Gospel, is the subconscious desire to please people. What must not die is the will to love people for the sake of Christ.

The parable does not end on a sad note. The fourth soil type "stands for those with a noble and good heart, who hear the word, retain it, and by persevering produce a crop." Judging by the numbers, Jesus was a failure. The large crowds were not taking in the Word of God and Jesus knew why. Yet, he was also confident that some would hear, retain, and persevere in the truth of the Gospel. Instead of seeing the crowds, Jesus saw the Twelve and "also some women who had been cured of evil spirits and diseases." These are the people he knew by name. There was Mary, "from whom seven demons had come out." Thankfully, demonic power had not been able to snatch the seed of the Gospel from the beaten path of Mary's life. There was Joanna, the wife of Cuza, the manager of Herod's household. By God's grace, the prestige and pressure of her husband's high position did not interfere with her acceptance of the Word of Truth. Praise God for Susanna, and many others. These women were financially supporting Jesus and his inner circle of disciples out of their own means. They heard, obeyed, and persevered in the Gospel.

For Jesus, nothing other than hearing and obeying the Word of God can bring us together as the family of God. Luke closes

---

23. P. T. Forsyth, "The Ideal Ministry," *The British Congregationalist*, October 18, 1906; quoted in *The Art of Pastoring*, David Hansen (Downers Grove, Ill.: IVP, 1994), p. 37.

this section with a reaction from Jesus that speaks volumes, if we care to listen. "Now Jesus' mother and brothers came to see him, but they were not able to get near because of the crowd. Someone told him, `Your mother and brothers are standing outside, wanting to see you.' He replied, `My mother and brothers are those who hear God's word and put it into practice.'" There are many shared experiences and affinities that bring us together, but for most people the strongest bond is family. The family ranks above generational and professional affinities. But for Jesus the natural bond of the biological family was not the foundation for true community. The real and enduring bond between people was not generational, regional, professional, biological, or social. The true and lasting bond between people is rooted in listening to and living out the Word of God. This is what it means to abide in Christ and this is what it means to be rooted and established in love.[24] Are we listening to God? Really listening?

A JOSIAH STORY

Josiah's story, like David's psalm and Jesus' parable, under- scores what it means to receive the text.[25] Josiah shines as a bright light in an otherwise bleak period of Israel's history. It is still breaking news when someone says, "I have found the Word of God" and really means it. For as in the days of Josiah, the Word lies buried, not under a pile of rubble, but under the weight of intellectual suspicion, religious pride, feelings of secular superiority, spiritual apathy, or just plain laziness. When Hilkiah the high priest said to Shaphan the secretary of

---

24. John 15; Ephesians 3:17.
25. 2 Kings 22:1-23:30.

state, "I have found the Book of the Law in the temple of the Lord," he knew he was onto something important. News of the discovery traveled up the chain of command to the king, but not before Shaphan read the Book of the Law for himself. The biblical account unfolds with a growing sense of tension as the secretary reads from the book in the presence of the 26-year-old king. We cannot help but wonder what Josiah's response is going to be.

Josiah's predecessor, King Manasseh, reigned for fifty-five years and during that time someone decided to put the Law of God in storage. The book may have been deemed irrelevant because of the king's aggressive campaign to open Judah up to religious pluralism and an array of exciting new spiritualities promoted by the surrounding nations. Manasseh brought about sweeping changes—devastating changes. He introduced fertility cults, child sacrifice, and placed foreign idols in the temple. No wonder the Book of the Law lay forgotten for decades until Hilkiah the high priest discovered it. When Josiah came to power at the age of eight, he inherited a spiritual disaster of staggering proportions. Eighteen years later Josiah initiated a renovation of the temple that led to the rediscovery of the first five books of the Old Testament. Shaphan, the secretary of state, rather than Hilkiah the high priest, read from the book in the presence of King Josiah. Imagine Josiah hearing for the first time Moses' sermons in the Book of Deuteronomy.[26] Josiah's story has lasting impact because he heard the Word of God. His hearing set in motion a chain-reaction of repentance, fierce public action, and joyful celebration. Josiah was demonstrative. He tore his robes in heartfelt repentance and called for

---

26. Deuteronomy 4:1-4, 9, 23-27.

the prophet Huldah. His responsiveness to the Word of God ignited a national renewal movement, the likes of which Judah had not seen for 75 years. King Josiah took decisive action. He called all the leaders and all the people together, "from the least to the greatest" and "he read in their hearing all the words of the Book of the Covenant."[27] He stood by the pillar in the temple and "renewed the covenant in the presence of the Lord," with words right out of Deuteronomy.[28] Josiah's reading of the Law led him to deconstruct the culture. Overnight, Jerusalem's embrace of all things pagan, including tolerance for religious pluralism and encouragement of sexual rituals, was rejected and destroyed. Josiah had all the articles and objects used for honoring Baal and Asherah and all the starry hosts removed from the temple. He tore down the quarters for the male prostitutes and all the trappings of the fertility cults. He desecrated Topheth (meaning 'incinerator') where children were sacrificed in a raging fire to Molech, a Canaanite deity. Symbols of power and success, such as horses and chariots dedicated to the sun, were destroyed, along with the high places dedicated to religious pluralism. What I find especially impressive about Josiah's story is the torrent of activity unleashed because he heard the Word of God. He removed, scattered, slaughtered, smashed, pulled down, and burned up any and everything that violated the Word of God. Only then, did the king give orders to all the people to celebrate the Passover.

We have a Text. The search is over. Accessibility is not the issue, but intelligibility is. Exposure is everywhere, but internalization is rare. Like Augustine in his famous conversion

---

27. 2 Kings 23:2.
28. Deuteronomy 6:5, 17.

story all we need to do is pick it up and read it. Really read it! Yet hearing the Word of the Lord is hard to do. We are hard of hearing and our lives are hardened to the Gospel. Let God open up your ears and dig through the pile of distractions. Let the Holy Spirit turn down the volume on those competing voices. Cease the scanning, surfing, and skipping, long enough to let the seed of the Gospel take deep root. Forget the old way of rummaging through the junk yard of pop culture, trying to cobble together a worldview. Instead of tinkering, embrace the Word of God. Let the Text shape the subtext of your life, and not the other way around. Pray the psalm, "Sacrifice and offering you did not desire—but my ears you have opened." Heed the parable. The secrets of the kingdom of God have been given to you. Listen up! Identify with Josiah. Let the Word deconstruct your life, whether it is miserable or nice, and lead you to repentance and action. We have the Text. The Word of the Lord. Thanks be to God.

3

FINITE TEXT/INFINITE TRUTH

On the road to Emmaus, Jesus had a conversation about the story of salvation history. He did it at a walking pace for about seven miles. "And beginning with Moses and all the Prophets, he explained to them what was said in all the Scriptures concerning himself."[1] I wish we had this conversation verbatim, but even if we did, it wouldn't add anything to what we already know from the Word of God. However, what a wonderful experience it must have been for these two disciples to have Jesus explain "all the Scriptures concerning himself." The conversation may have included:

Abel's sacrificial lamb, Abraham at the altar with Isaac, Job's cry, "I know that my Redeemer lives and that in the end he will stand on the earth and after my skin has been destroyed yet in my flesh I will see him,"

Israel's Passover lamb, Moses raising the serpent in the wilderness,

---

1. Luke 24:27.

David's prayer, "My God, my God, why have you forsaken me?"

Isaiah's picture of the suffering servant, Daniel's vision of the victorious Son of Man,

and Zechariah's humble king, unappreciated shepherd, and the mourned martyr.

"And beginning with Moses and all the Prophets" takes the whole account in from Genesis to Malachi. Preachers have the opportunity to bring people into that conversation and give them a taste of that experience.

We hold the finite text in tension with infinite truth. Jesus surveyed the biblical narrative in the time it took to walk to Emmaus and drew out its salvation-making, history-changing, life-transforming significance. The two disciples felt the impact of the Word of God rightly divided: "Were not our hearts burning within us while he talked with us on the road and opened the Scriptures to us?"[2]

There is an unnecessary mystique that surrounds the Bible that keeps even earnest believers from grasping its meaning. We make the text out to be unwieldy and complicated. We have parsed, translated, exegeted, researched, debated, and interpreted the text, to the point of abstraction and learned sophistry. Paradoxically, we have reduced the text to sound bites, power point outlines and anecdotal illustrations. Bad sermons give the impression that the Bible is a moralistic storybook or a guide for self-help or a resource for motivational speakers. Poor scholarship gives the impression that the Bible is undependable, fraught with wild and strange variants and competing, contradictory ideas. Many churchgoing readers see the Bible as a huge undifferentiated mass of spiritual material

---

2. Luke 24:32.

designed to inspire devotional daily thoughts or they see it as The Good Book with secrets for success and stories of courage. For others, the Bible has the same aura as the Islamic Koran or the Hindus Vedas—a strange religious document best interpreted by experts.

"For most people in our culture," writes Bryan Chapell, "the Bible is an opaque book whose truths are hidden in an endless maze of difficult words, unfamiliar history, unpronounceable names, and impenetrable mysticism."[3] He counters this common fallacy, by insisting that "the best preachers guide in such a way that their listeners discover that the labyrinth is a myth. There are no dark passageways through twisted mazes of logic to biblical truth that require the expertise of the spiritual elite. There is only a well-worn path than anyone can follow if a preacher sheds some ordinary light along the way."[4]

Explanation and understanding are not as elusive as they are made out to be. Through the simple tasks of observing what is going on in the text, asking basic questions, and relating the text to real people we can grasp the biblical message. "Excellent preaching makes people confident that biblical truth lies within their reach, not beyond their grasp."[5]

What Jesus did in seven miles on the way to Emmaus, Stephen did in seven minutes in his speech to the Sanhedrin.[6] In the wisdom of the Spirit, Stephen boldly proclaimed the gospel according to Abraham, Joseph, Moses, and Solomon. He declared the Story in the midst of an angry Sanhedrin. It

---

3. Bryan Chapell, *Christ-Centered Preaching: Redeeming the Expository Sermon* (Grand Rapids, MI: Baker, 2005), p. 103.
4. Chapell, p. 103.
5. Chapell, p. 110.
6. Acts 7

cost him his life, but he gave them their history, grounded in a finite text, pointing to their crucified Messiah. This finite text has parameters—fixed limits. The message is vast; the truth exceeds our grasp. We will never exhaust it, but the Bible has only so many pages—1,137 in my Bible.

We have to find ways to grasp this finite text if we expect to proclaim its infinite meaning. Jesus did. Stephen did. All the biblical writers did. Beautiful music relies on twelve pitches. The artist works with a palate of five primary colors. The Periodic Table is made of 92 natural elements. The English language uses 26 letters. The Bible is knowable: its literary forms are recognizable; its history is manageable; and its revelation of God is comprehensible—truth we never would have imagined or invented.

TABLE OF CONTENTS

Open up your Bible to the table of contents and you see 66 books listed in order of their purpose and genre. The first five books are commonly known as The Books of Moses and are foundational to the rest of the Bible. They tell the story of God's creation of the world, from the cosmos to the first human couple and from the nations to the covenant people of Israel. God conceives, redeems, identifies, and gathers a people for himself to be a blessing to the nations. Twelve history books follow, from Joshua to Esther, charting the course of this tiny beleaguered people through Israel's early history. Then, the Wisdom Books explore the human experience in relationship to God and each other: Job, Psalms, Proverbs, Ecclesiastes, and Song of Songs. The rest of the Old Testament is made up of prophets, sixteen of them from Isaiah to Malachi. The prophets are confrontational. Their job is to declare the judgment of God against all sin and rebellion and the salvation of God for all those who turn to God in humility, repentance and faith. The tension in the text is between judgment and salvation—between the fallen condition focus and God's redemptive provision.

The New Testament consists of five stories, twenty-one letters, and one visionary poem. The Four Gospels place Jesus in the context of all that has gone before. He is the culmination and climax of all the Law and the Prophets. Everything points to him. They tell the story of Jesus in the street language of the day. Matthew, Mark, Luke and John use the Jesus way to communicate, his personal encounters, parables, miracles, and messages. They take us to the cross and the empty tomb. Acts tells us the story of Christ and the early church. Luke picks up the narrative of the risen Lord Jesus and describes how the church grew from Jerusalem to Rome. The twenty-one letters give apostolic shape to the emerging mission of God. All their theology is practical. Nothing is esoteric and abstract. Everything involves the day-to-day life of the church on the move. Sin and salvation, worship and judgment, mission and love get worked out in the real world. No one is playing church or going through the motions. St. John's Revelation brings the canon to an end. In the Spirit, he orchestrates a powerful symphony of countervailing tensions, worship and judgment, judgment and worship.

To our human imagination space is limitless. When we begin talking about so many light years to the nearest star, we begin to lose track of time. But human history is not like cosmic space. Day to day living is still framed the same old-fashioned way from sun rise to sun rise. Twenty-four hours in a day, 365 days in a year, 10 years in a decade, 100 years in a century, a 1000 years in a millennium, and before you know it you've counted up human history. Time frames human history on planet earth within parameters we can understand. Think of it this way: my grandfather lived to 93. Just twenty or so generations of people who lived like my grandfather to a ripe old age, and we're back to the time of Christ's resurrection. Biblical history, which is to say human history, has a knowable time line. It is not a black hole of limitless time, even if we may feel that way in history class.

Only Genesis 1–11 covers a span of time too long for us to take in. Dating the cosmos is anyone's guess, because we have no idea of the time lapse in Genesis one. For all we know it may have been billions of years. Adam begins human history, but Abraham is our historical key for dating, somewhere around 2000 to 1800 BC. Three generations of Patriarchs, Isaac, Jacob, and Joseph, cover two hundred years in Canaan, followed by 430 years of bondage in Egypt. Moses and the Exodus dates from somewhere around 1450 BC. Forty years of wilderness wanderings precedes Joshua's conquest of Canaan in 1400 BC. The history of the Judges from Othniel to Samson covers another 400 years. David, the great grandson of Ruth, was fully established on the throne of Israel by 1000 BC. Following his son Solomon's reign, Israel was divided into two kingdoms in 931 BC. Jeroboam in the north and Rehoboam in the south. From the divided kingdom to the fall of Jerusalem in 586, we have two long lists of 38 kings split between Samaria and Judah. During this time, the major players are the prophets, along with Ezra, Esther and Nehemiah. Listed in chronological order they appear as follows: Joel, Jonah, Amos, Hosea, Isaiah, Micah, Habakkuk, Zephaniah, Jeremiah, Ezekiel, Daniel, Ezra (1-10), Haggai, Zechariah, Ezra (6-19), Esther, Nehemiah, Malachi. Between Malachi's prophecy of the coming Lord and its fulfillment in Jesus stands another 400 years, remarkable for their canonical silence.[7] The main contours of this time line are easy to remember, even if it is difficult to remember the names of the kings and the order of the prophets. At times the line of salvation history seems to grow perilously thin, but the theology of God's promise and provision abide forever.

The chronology of the New Testament is altogether different. These five stories, twenty-one letters, and one visionary poem were all written in the first century. Mark may have been the first gospel account, followed by Matthew, Luke-Acts, and John. The Fourfold Gospel covers the span of Jesus' life, concentrating on the three years of his public ministry. What is surprising is that a third of the gospel is devoted to the week of his passion, death and resurrection. The span of salvation history stretching thousands of years narrows down to this one week in time that is absolutely pivotal for all that preceded and all that follows. The apostle Paul was probably the first to put pen to paper, when he wrote Thessalonians in the early 50s, followed by Galatians, 1 Corinthians, Philippians, 2 Corinthians, Romans, Colossians, Ephesians, 1 Timothy, Titus, and 2 Timothy. Paul's letters span a little over a decade, assuming that Paul died in Rome sometime in the mid to late 60s. Presumably, the Book of Hebrews was written in the 60s, prior to the destruction of the temple in 70 AD since the book seems to assume the levitical priesthood was going strong. James may have written his letter shortly before his martyrdom in AD 62. Peter's two letters were probably written shortly before the Neronian persecution in AD 64. Jude may have been written between 66 and 70. The letters of John and the Book of Revelation may date from the

---

7. Malachi 3:1; Matthew 11:10.

90s. In the space of forty years we have our New Testament, a finite text with infinite meaning. We cannot help but think of the real incarnation of our Lord every time we open the Bible. The Word made flesh, entered our neighborhood, and chose the limitations of human language and history to make known his grace and truth.

TAPESTRY OF TRUTH

As we said earlier, texture is the art of weaving a story into the text. The thoughtful reader comes to appreciate the finiteness of the biblical text through the rich and dynamic interplay of resounding themes. Given this diversity of genres and expanse of time, we might expect a collection of spiritual materials, catalogued and compartmentalized, but what we have in Scripture "is a vast tapestry of God's creating, saving and blessing ways in the world."[8] In the Spirit, the whole Word of God ties together beautifully. Yet this convergence of meaning and networking of truth is not on display in some overtly obvious way. It cannot be reduced to paint-by-number simplicity or power point bullets. There is nothing clever or ingenious or contrived about this weaving together of biblical truth. We want to be careful not to impose our own ideas onto the biblical text. We want to read the text, pray over it, and meditate on the meaning, so that these relationships emerge from within without being forced on the text.

Hebrew poetry rhymes themes not sounds. Parallel lines nuance and enhance the truth from different angles. The

---

8. Eugene H. Peterson, *The Message Remix* (Colorado Springs, CO: NavPress, 2003), p. 287.

praying poet repeats a single idea from a variety of perspectives. Psalm 19 is a good example:

> The law of the Lord is perfect,
>   refreshing the soul,
> The statutes of the Lord are trustworthy,
>   making wise the simple.
> The precepts of the Lord are right,
>   giving joy to the heart.

Within the canon of Scripture there is a truth-enhancing parallelism. The biblical authors were aware of this weaving together of themes. In some cases, these truth-connections are intentional, other times they appear to be unintentional, but in every instance they are consistent with the ultimate authorship of the Spirit of Christ. Revelation as a whole reflects the unity of a singular truth resounding through the dynamic redemptive meta-narrative. There is nothing prosaic or pedantic about it. The Bible is not a literary artifact, but Salvation's Story. Compressing the biblical data into information packages of dates, details, doctrines and dissected passages robs the text of its tension, tone, texture and tapestry. Our aptitude for de-constructing the passion and poetry of the faith into nouns of abstraction needs to be re-thought. Virtual preaching may be streaming live on-line, but a steady diet of it disembodies the gospel, de-incarnates the faith and produces a virtual congregation.

The apostle John was intentional about linking his gospel account to Genesis. John's first line, "In the beginning was the Word," parallels Moses' first line, "In the beginning God created the heavens and the earth." The connection between the poetic overture of Genesis and the prologue of John extends to the entire Pentateuch ("five volume book") and the first five books of the New Testament. Exodus and Mark form a natural connection. Salvation is on the move. Action and immediacy shape the narrative. God is at work in concrete, history-changing ways. Leviticus and Numbers link with Matthew's Gospel. These two Old Testament books trained the people of God in holiness and organized them into a believing community. Matthew's emphasis on Jesus' teaching put new wine in old skins, fulfilling the Law and reshaping the people of God into a family. Deuteronomy, Moses' community-forming sermon series, resonants with Luke's missional story of Jesus and his church. No one who follows Jesus is a spectator or an admirer, everyone is a disciple, marked by the cross, involved in the church, gifted by the Spirit and engaged in mission.

The fourfold gospel is tightly woven with all that has gone before. The genealogies, encounters, sermons, parables, miracles, and passion week are all grounded in what has gone before. Joshua leading the people into the promised land parallels Paul proclaiming the gospel to the Gentiles. The era of Judges, when everyone did what was right in their own eyes links with Paul's freedom epistle to the Galatians. Mary reminds us of Hannah and Samuel links us to John the Baptist. The first and last Old Testament prophets go together. Israel in her insistence on a king foreshadows the Pharisees' expectation of a political messiah. King David's life parallels the life of Jesus the Son of David. I'm not suggesting that the Bible is a jigsaw puzzle. It's not a game, designed for us to fit the pieces together. But any reader can begin to line up the Story and make the natural connections and the more this is done the more we see the truth in high definition.

Peter's letters recall the story of Ruth in a way that is far deeper than mere illustration. "Once you were not a people, but now you are the people of God," describes what God has done and intends to do. Ruth and Peter stand as unlikely candidates for playing leading roles in salvation history, and in that capacity they represent us—ordinary believers who put their trust in the God of all salvation. The collaborative nature of this truth-telling Story emphasizes the mercy of God. The four stories of Hannah, Samuel, Saul and David scale the drama of salvation down to real people who either receive or resist the mercy of God. They prepare us for the gospel encounters and our encounter with Jesus. The Books of Kings and Chronicles raise the issue of God's sovereignty. More than forty kings depict the mess of the human condition and the lostness of humankind. All the king's men and all the king's horses can't put life back together again. These ancient accounts form a counterpoint to the apostle Paul's celebration in the Book of Ephesians of God's electing, predestinating, and redeeming sovereignty.

Leadership grounded in the Word of God links Ezra with Paul's letters to Timothy and Nehemiah's "joy of the Lord is our strength" recalls Paul's epistle of joy, Philippians. Esther fits beautifully with Philemon. God's salvation works into local history and liberates slaves. The gospel is more political than we expected but in a way that no one imagines.

It is for good reason that the five Wisdom Books form the center of the canon. They belong in the New Testament as much as the Old. They remain as vital to the 21st century disciple of Jesus as they did to God's people in Babylonian captivity. When seen as a unit with the Psalms at the center and two sets of polarities, Job and Proverbs, Ecclesiastes and Song of Songs, crisscrossing the center, we begin to understand their essential impact on life.

Psalms is a magnetic center, pulling every scrap and dimension of human experience into the presence of God . . . The Job-Proverbs polarity sets the crisis experience of extreme suffering opposite the routine experience of getting along as best we can in the ordinary affairs of work and family, money and sex, the use of language and the expression of emotions . . . The Song-Ecclesiastes polarity sets the ecstatic experience of love in tension with the boredom of the same round. The life of faith has to do with the glories of discovering far more in life than we ever dreamed of; the life of faith has to do with doggedly putting one flat foot in front of the other, wondering what the point of it all is.[9]

There is an immensity to the Prophets that can be intimidating and a message that refuses to be domesticated. Efforts to package the prophets for easy consumption fail. Unfamiliar people and places, obscure metaphors and subtle meanings can cause the reader to give up, but the ordinary disciple cannot afford to neglect these fiery prophets who fuse complexity and simplicity. The prophets never leave any doubt in our minds as to their intended message of hope and salvation no matter how many historical details and literary allusions may miss us. The deep affinity between Jesus and the prophets makes them mandatory for spiritual formation and ethical obedience. Sixteen prophets and twelve disciples symbolize the tapestry of truths woven into this finite text. Isaiah anchors the prophets as Romans anchors Paul's letters. The Book of Jeremiah corresponds well with Paul's Corinthian correspondence, as it wrestles with the integrity of God's Word among religious professionals who think they know better. Ezekiel and Daniel prepare us for the cryptic visions of the Book of Revelation. Daniel and Colossians revive our sense of a God-centric

---

9. Eugene Peterson, *The Message Remix*, p. 527.

cosmos. In a world filled with competing spiritual and political forces, a Jewish exile in Babylon and a Jewish apostle to the Gentiles, argue calmly and persuasively for the convergence of all things in Christ. Hosea's love story fits with John's letters on love. Both the prophets and the apostles delve into the meaning of the love of God and loving one another. Amos' fiery message of judgment and his attack on solemn assemblies resonants with the Book of Hebrews. Like Amos the author of Hebrews argues against traditional religion and calls for true reverence and awe, "for our 'God is a consuming fire.'"

Micah's call "to act justly and to love mercy and to walk humbly with your God" fits well with James' down-to-earth working faith. The Book of Malachi passionately sought to prepare the people of God for the first Advent. The prophet was worked-up against their apathy and disobedience. He wanted to put the fear-of-the-Lord in them. Likewise, Paul earnestly sought to reassure the church of the coming Day of the Lord in 1 & 2 Thessalonians. He challenged the church to work hard, remain faithful, and to live in hope of the coming of the Lord. As I said earlier, the point here is not to connect-the-dots or impose a grid on the Bible. The point is to pay attention to the resounding themes of truth in Salvation's symphony.

Dale Bruner's masterful two-volume commentary on the Gospel of Matthew runs nearly fifteen hundred pages.[10] It is what a commentary should be: conversant with ancient and modern scholarship, linguistically accurate, textually astute, theologically comprehensive, and ethically aware. Bruner's highly readable work is rooted in the canon of Scripture, filled

---

10. Dale Brunner, *Matthew: A Commentary*, vols. 1-2 (Grand Rapids, MI: Eerdmans, 2004).

with pastoral insights, devotional reflection, and relevant application for the church. But as good as Bruner's commentary is, no one would ever claim that the final commentary on Matthew has been written. All of our work on the text is open-ended. Unfinished. We will never be done with the task of studying, interpreting, and applying the Word of God, but the text itself is finite. We can grasp its genres, mark its history, and begin to comprehend its meaning. Ordinary believers, like you and me, can be shaped and guided by the whole counsel of God. With study and prayer we can be at home in this text.

By the time Jesus arrived in Emmaus he had given these two disciples an understanding of Scripture like they had never heard before. In less than seven miles, he had set their hearts on fire with the Word of God. We have been given a finite text to read, study, and preach so that the body of Christ might be thoroughly equipped for every good work.[11]

FINITE WORLD

A word of caution is in order. We don't want to squeeze this finite text into our finite world. To be at home in the biblical text has nothing to do with fitting the Bible into our lives. All of our efforts to systematize and package the Word, box-it-up for easy consumption, and domesticate it for our convenience,

---

11. Two quotes placed side-by-side from Eugene Peterson's *Eat This Book* help illustrate the goal and the danger in handling this finite text: (1) "What I want to call attention to is the Bible, all of it, is livable; it is *the* text for living our lives. It reveals a God-created, God-ordered, God-blessed world in which we find ourselves at home and whole" (p.18). (2) "But nothing in our Bibles is one-dimensional, systematized, or theologized. Everything in the text is intimately and organically linked to lived reality. We can no more diagram and chart the Bible into neatly labeled subjects or developments than we can our gardens" (p.65).

will meet with success. But it is not the kind of success we need nor want. We face a tendency to use the Bible to defend and sanctify our material and political world. Instead of being shaped by the drama of salvation history, we are tempted to mold the Bible into a self-help manual or a manifesto for the American Dream. We say we take the Bible seriously, that we interpret it literally and defend its inerrancy, but then we proceed to reduce the Bible to a systematic theology of useful information and platitudinous ten easy steps to successful living. Preachers attract tens of thousands of unsuspecting Christians with their prosperity gospel, snatching a verse here and a verse there, to demonstrate that the Bible is on their side. But what they are really doing is abusing the Bible, using it for their own ends. They may be our most glaring examples of cramming the text into their finite world, but we do the same thing when we reduce the Bible to a mental exercise or to a devotional experience. Both scholarship and sentiment can be used to distance ourselves from the Word of God. God invites us into his immense salvation-shaped world, not the world of our peace and prosperity, but the world of God's mission, the world where Christ reigns over every sphere of life, the world that leads to our cross and our resurrection. The Living Word calls us out of the small world of our own making and into the large, grace-filled world of God's making.

Jesus accused the religious leaders of his day of possessing the Scriptures but not hearing the voice of God: "You have never heard his voice nor seen his form nor does his word dwell in you, for you do not believe the one he sent. You study the Scriptures diligently because you think that in them you possess eternal life. These are the very Scriptures that testify about me, yet you refuse to come to me to have life."[12] Jesus said this to men steeped in the Scriptures, who had memorized large portions of Scripture. They loved the Books of Moses and held them as dear as anyone could hold anything dear. But they still didn't get it. Their finite world of religious ritual, tradition, and compliance with the law had become an end itself. They did not hear the voice of God. Instead of being transformed by the Word of God, they shaped and molded the Bible into their image. They never internalized the message or read the Bible along its prophetic trajectory. Instead of participating in the drama of salvation history, they stood apart from it, detached, disengaged, and ultimately against the Bible.

These first century technicians of the text had exegeted the Bible from every angle imaginable, listing and debating every possible interpretation. They were constantly deciphering and decoding the most inscrutable aspects of the text, but they did not see how any of it connected to Jesus. A technician breaks down the finite text into its various parts and puts these items on display for debate and exhibition. Some exegetes treat the biblical text like a crime scene. They pull out their forensics kits to discover the secret problems of the text. However, a true textuary delves into the finite text and enters into its drama, knowing not only the technical aspects of a biblical passage, but its sense and meaning. Textuaries eat, digest and metabolize the Word of God so that it becomes a part of them. Instead of sitting in judgment on the text, textuaries have entered into the Story. Instead of their personal stories and finite world overshadowing the finite text, God's Story redeems their story.

---

12. John 5:37-40

4

STORIED TEXT

On a visit to northern Ghana, I learned that one of the most important positions in the Janga tribe is that of "linguist." Second only to the chief, the tribal linguist is responsible for telling the story of his people. Like the chief, his position is inherited by birth. He carries the responsibility of being the tribe's spokesperson, the chief's advisor, and, most important, the guardian of the tribe's oral history. Normally a "linguist" refers to a person who is an expert in languages, one who analyzes the syntax, structure, and systematicity of languages. Linguists can decipher a language and break it down into its component parts. Through careful study they know how a given language works. But the term *linguist* in Ghana applies to a person who *uses* language to communicate, rather than observes how language is used. The tribal linguist is more of a poet than a technician.

To the delight of the gathered crowd, the linguist danced his way from the chief to our visiting delegation, transforming protocol into a memorable event. Anyone could tell that he enjoyed the art of communication and everybody agreed he really knew how to tell the story. He used his poetic flair, personal charisma and passion to proclaim the history of his people. Janga's tribal linguist is a picture to me of what the followers of the Lord Jesus are to become. We are to be God's linguists. We are, in Paul's words, to "guard what has been entrusted to [our] care." We are to "turn away from godless chatter and the opposing ideas of what is falsely called knowledge."[1] We are to do our best to present ourselves to God as true craftsmen, who do not need to be ashamed and who correctly handle the word of truth.[2] Jude urged us "to contend for the faith that was once for all entrusted to the saints."[3] The analogy seemed to work well for the African pastors, who readily embraced the idea of being God's linguists.

Like the Janga linguist we are born into our responsibility. "For you have been born again, not of perishable seed, but of imperishable, through the living and enduring Word of God." Peter continued with a word from the prophet Isaiah, "All people are like grass, and all their glory is like the flowers of the field; the grass withers and the flowers fall, but the word of the Lord stands forever."[4] When the people of Janga see their tribal linguist, they see so much more than a little old man. They see their history, their tradition, and their culture. In fact, they see even more, they see the pride of their history, the meaning of their tradition and the joy of their culture. Isn't this how it should be with us? God meant for our lives to embody the gospel message, so that when people see us they see Christ.

---

1.   1 Timothy 6:20
2.   2 Timothy 2:15
3.   Jude 3
4.   1 Peter 1:23-25

The ministry of the Word requires that we comprehend more deeply the drama of God's great salvation history. This is an approach to the Bible that I would have benefitted from at the beginning of my formal theological education. Like so many Bible and theology students I started out by taking language studies and courses in theology and hermeneutics. I enjoyed classes that delved into background information on the text and explored the latest critical studies. I studied works by famous biblical scholars and theologians and did research on higher criticism, form criticism, and the historical-grammatical method of biblical interpretation. I found these courses and my professors fascinating. In fact there was very little in the graduate school curriculum that I didn't enjoy or imagine myself teaching someday. I liked it all: biblical and historical theology, church history, evangelism, and missions. But I was unaware of something missing in my theological education and ministry preparation until years later. I spent several years studying theological German and Latin and exploring every facet of Latin American Liberation Theology. I read Augustine for the better part of an academic year and sat under brilliant scholars, but I could not have explained to you the importance of the prophet Zechariah or the impact of Isaiah. I knew the trends of modern theology better than I knew God's salvation history.

I grew up in a home that practiced the spiritual disciplines and encouraged a devotional life. For family devotions we read from *The Daily Bread* and a short passage of Scripture that the devotional guide recommended. In my personal devotions I read Oswald Chambers and kept a journal of my daily Bible reading. Thanks to my parents who lived out the kingdom lifestyle long before it was called that in popular evangelicalism, I was nurtured and instructed in a home that embraced the Word of God. But I still didn't have a sense of the big picture of salvation history. Much of the Old Testament was foreign to me, like the old and forgotten stuff that got stored in our attic. I heard a zillion evangelistic messages at our church, but almost nothing from the biblical prophets.

During my junior high years our pastor focused almost exclusively on the apostle Paul, but it was preaching through the narrow lens of our subculture, rather than the great drama of salvation history. I knew a lot about "getting saved" but not a whole lot about the comprehensive meaning of salvation. Looking back, I sense that my family had an intuitive grasp of the message of the prophets and Jesus' kingdom ethic, but I didn't see how it all fit together. I had pieces of the puzzle but not the big picture. Except for a few well-known psalms, the riches of the Bible's Wisdom literature were lost to me. Biblical books, such as Leviticus or Numbers, were basically ignored or, when thought about at all, regarded as anachronisms for New Testament Christians. Forays into confusing books like Ezekiel or Daniel were usually for the sake of discovering a devotional thought for the day. I used the book of Revelation to fuel my curiosity more than to deepen my courage.

Although good in themselves, my devotional experience of the Word and my graduate theological education conspired to conceal my ignorance of the sweep and drama of salvation history. My experience and my scholarship produced an unintended and hidden deficiency—an inability to see the big picture and feel the drama of God's story. My well-intentioned devotional subjectivity and specialized expertise had unwittingly obscured the Gospel story. I was left with a piecemeal understanding of the Bible and at the time it didn't bother me that large portions of the Bible remained relatively unknown to me. What I was missing was a coherent understanding of the compelling unity of the Word of God.

Comprehending the fullness of the Gospel story is imperative for learning how to preach the truth. No matter how much preachers attend to the clarity of their thoughts and the effectiveness of their style, if the driving force of God's truth is not shaping their message then they are bound to fail, even if their sermons are well-received. Students come to divinity school to learn how to tell the Gospel story from cover to cover, but this is where we often disappoint students. By focusing on prolegomena and technical issues, at the expense of the big picture, seminaries have a way of exhausting students and preventing them from understanding the scope of God's work. Good teachers know this and guard against it. They defy the scribal propensity to overwhelm students with the complexities and intricacies of scholarly opinions. Their primary purpose is positive: to guide students in the powerful story of God's revelation. Their goal is not to debunk students of their intellectual naivete. There is a place for careful explanation, where interpretations are weighed, scholarly debates reviewed, and the latest research cited, but spiritual formation works best when the flow of salvation history is understood.

Wisdom dictates that we first hear the story before dissecting the text. By the time many divinity students plow through the scholarly introduction of a biblical book, including authorship, sources, date, setting, redaction criticism, exegetical problems, etc., they have lost the intellectual and spiritual energy to hear the story, much less proclaim it! These academic questions and concerns can be important, but their priority should be reversed. Begin with the story, revel in the truth and when once that storied truth is internalized in the soul, turn to the textual technicalities and complexities. Students find it difficult to proclaim what they have been trained to see as problematic. To use an analogy, seminary professors are trying to teach advanced auto mechanics to people who haven't even gotten their driver's license. Textual experts need to be careful with the biblical story. Their love of grammar and syntax may cause them to miss the tone and texture, and especially the truth of this real life story. Scholars can exegete a biblical passage, and pastors can work up sermons, but never really tell the story and embrace the message.

In her essay, "The Catholic Novelist in the South," Flannery O'Conner distinguishes between a correctable deficiency and invincible ignorance. Meaning—specifically Christian meaning—can once again be restored if we rediscover the biblical story. "Abstractions, formulas, laws, will not do here. We have to have stories. It takes a story to make a story. . . .Our response to life is different if we have been taught only a definition of faith than it is if we have trembled with Abraham as he held the knife over Isaac. Both of these kinds of knowledge are necessary, but in the last four or five centuries we in the Church have overemphasized the abstract and consequently impoverished our imagination and our capacity for prophetic insight. . . .We enjoy indulging ourselves in the logic that kills, in making categories smaller and smaller, in prescribing subjects and proscribing attitudes."[5]

Not only do we want to begin in the biblical story but we want to remain in this story throughout our ministry. "Within

---

5. Flannery O'Conner, *Collected Works* (New York: The Library Press of America, 1988) pp. 858-859.

this large, capacious context of the biblical story," Eugene Peterson writes,

> we learn to think accurately, behave morally, preach passionately, and sing joyfully, pray honestly, obey faithfully. But we dare not abandon the story as we go off and do any or all of these things, for the minute we abandon the story we go off and reduce reality to the dimensions of our minds and feelings and experience. The moment we formulate our doctrines, draw up our moral codes, and throw ourselves into a life of discipleship and ministry apart from a continuous re-immersing in the story itself, we walk right out of the concrete and local presence and activity of God and set up our own shop.[6]

A great deal of preaching tends to be piecemeal and heavily reliant on incidental anecdotal material. Preachers unintentionally interrupt God's Story with their own human interest stories and doctrinal expositions. It is time we concentrate on that compelling, convicting, lifesaving Story.

In *The Courage to Teach*, Parker Palmer insists that all good teachers discover the DNA of a text. There is a core truth that needs to be understood to make sense of all the data. The "inner logic" of the text "contains the information necessary to reconstruct the whole—if it is illuminated by a laser, a highly organized beam of light. That laser is the act of teaching." Palmer continues,

> No matter what great thing we are studying, there is always an equivalent to the stem section under the microscope. In every great novel, there is a passage that when deeply understood, reveals how the author develops character, establishes tension,

---

6. Eugene H. Peterson, *Christ Plays in Ten Thousand Places* (Grand Rapids, MI: Eerdmans, 2005), p. 182.

creates dramatic movement. With that understanding, the student can read the rest of the novel insightfully.[7]

Preachers embrace the *scope* of the whole counsel of God and the *strategy* of discovering the tension in the text in order to explore the internal dynamic of the biblical text. We need to live in the Story and find out what's going on in the text!

What we must not do is forsake the text, but this is precisely what happens Sunday after Sunday. There is a text listed in the bulletin and this text is read to the congregation, but then we preachers smother the text in wordy preambles, small talk, human interest anecdotes, lengthy illustrations, evangelical cliches and moralistic platitudes. Preachers drown out the Word of God with Christian chatter—run-on repetitive thoughts that have been said a zillion times. "Cultivating a sense of narrativity has to be high on the list of pastoral urgencies in our day," insists Eugene Peterson.

> There is no one so well-placed in our American culture as the pastor to counter the fragmenting forces of our age that reduce us to a pile of emotional shards and disconnected ideas. Who else has the chance to speak weekly to the same gathering of people in a personal way in the context of both their lives and life of Jesus—the two commanding stories that we inhabit. I regret that so many pastors squander the vitalities of story and Story, in which the pulpit and parish are so rich, for the 'inspirational' insipidities of power point.[8]

Years ago, when I was on the staff of a mega-church, the pastoral team, seven of us, met once a week for breakfast. The

---

7. Parker Palmer, *The Courage to Teach*, p. 123
8. Eugene Peterson, personal correspondence, February 4, 2006.

designated refrain for the anecdotes and jokes that we thought good enough for prime time preaching was "That'll Preach!" We rarely discussed the text, but we were always on the look out for what might hold the attention of a restless audience. Sermons were built on the humorous anecdote or an emotional story, with the text added later. What is missing often in our preaching is any sense of "Thus says the Lord." What we tend to give is religious bubble speech—sermonic jargon. Words float above the preacher, like balloon speech in cartoons. Listening to us, people have the right to ask if preachers are not themselves bored with the text. We do so much talking without preaching. I picture the prophet Jeremiah sitting in the congregation with a scowl on his face waiting for the Word of God.

God's Story is far more compelling than our theological abstractions and anecdotal tales. Pastors have a "cover-to-cover" responsibility and a "tension-in-the-text" obligation to teach and preach the whole counsel of God.

5

TENSION IN THE TEXT

The tension in the text is found in the clash between the mystery of God and the mess of the human condition, between humanity's fallen condition and God's work of redemption. To the degree that we identify with Jesus, his person and his work, we live in this tension. But it is exactly this tension that we have largely lost in contemporary Christian communication. We have obscured the polarity of Jesus-like lowliness and worldly success. We have blended Jesus-centered truth and cultural correctness. Søren Kierkegaard called this state, "Christianity without Christ." The Christianity of his day had taken on a life of its own—divorced from the message and method of Jesus. Instead of teaching people how to follow Jesus, preachers were enticing them to admire Jesus. There's a difference.

When the text loses its tension, Christian communication becomes repetitive, boring, and compatible with culture. Evading the text is not a regional issue as much as it is a national crisis. The problem exists in Bible-belt mega-churches and in avant-garde Emergent churches. The lack of real preaching is systemic to the American church from coast to coast, in all categories, rural, urban, and suburban. Denominational affiliation makes little difference and variety in worship styles does nothing to conceal the problem. There is a famine in the land, "not a famine of food or a thirst for water, but a famine of hearing the words of the Lord."[1]

Some time ago I heard a sermon on the theme "Abide in Christ" from John 15. The preacher appeared to do everything right. He gave a personable introduction, developed a logical outline, and delivered his sermon with emotion and energy. His points were clear (spend time in the Word, seek out Christian fellowship, obey the commandments, nurture friendships through love, etc.) yet nothing came through the sermon that gripped the soul. He gave us a recital of Christian assertions, a list of good things to do, but there was no tension in the text. His well-designed sermon seemed to evade the very meaning of the text that he sought to expound.

He chose not to pursue the obvious trinitarian challenge of the text ("I am the true vine and my Father is the gardener"). Perhaps he felt that connection would have been too demanding for us. Nor did he think it wise to link the imagery of the vine to its roots in salvation history, as a picture of Israel in rebellion. The prophets used this image to describe the unfruitful people of God.[2] "Abide in me" or "remain in me" implies an intensity that goes beyond mere belief. Believers are to be united to Christ in a way that will inevitably put us in conflict with our culture, even as Jesus was in his. What does it mean for us to be

---

1. Amos 8:11
2. Isaiah 5:1-7; Jeremiah 2:21

fruitful? Have we ever experienced unfruitfulness? These are the questions Jesus raised as he probed the lives of the disciples. This is the text that the Spirit of Christ uses to prune the dead branches of our lives and remove all obstacles to faithfulness and love. Jesus is confident that such a life of intimacy with him, obedience to the will of the Father, and love for others, will be so dominated by the kingdom of God that all our prayers will be answered. We will be in sync with the Lord Jesus.

The clear intent of the text is to probe our relationship with Christ. But the energetically delivered sermon gave no reason to think that our lives were in any way out of sync with an intimate relationship with Christ. People might have left the auditorium that day praising the pulpiteer for a masterful presentation, for delivering a well-crafted sermon, but I was upset. The way he spoke of Jesus reminded me of the stick-figure Jesus on an old-fashioned flannel-graph board. Anglican theologian and pastor Peter Jensen calls this "smooth preaching." The preacher covers "the main theme of a text but does not bring to the surface anything in the text that surprises, contradicts, creates tension. Smooth preaching rushes too easily to solutions, or more frequently, fails to see or fails to mention the stress points."[3] Over time smooth preaching "dulls the Word of God and fails to challenge."[4]

A few days later I asked a friend and Bible scholar, who attended the same service, what he got out of the sermon. He thought for a moment and said, "Well, nothing really, but the great thing about Joe is that he's always prepared. He preaches

---

3. Peter Jensen, "The Seminary and the Sermon," in *Preach The Word*, ed. Leland Ryken & Todd Wilson (Wheaton, IL: Crossway, 2007), p. 216.

4. Ibid.

Wednesday night, Sunday night, and leads a huge men's weekday Bible study. He always does a great job." I didn't say anything but I thought to myself what's the point of preaching three times a week if you don't really say anything? "Preaching that is comprehended only within the cloistered congregation of the knowledgeable, the well-informed, and the virtuously Christian is bound to be dull."[5]

Not too long ago I shifted cultures from southern California to the South and changed my primary responsibility. I moved from the weekly rhythm of preaching on Sunday to mentoring preachers in a divinity school. This change has had an impact on my listening. I used to listen with an ear for how the biblical text addressed specific, practical and personal questions in people's minds. From week to week, the issue was how does God's salvation history shape our lives? Where is the passion in this text? Now I am listening to successful preachers give sermons which seem to ignore these questions. They concentrate on relevant topics, moving or entertaining anecdotes, and practical steps to self-improvement. I hear a lot of topical sermons with lists of points and fill-in-the-blank answers. There is little tension in the text and the tension between Christ and culture is avoided except in ways that are non-controversial and unoffensive. Sermons are innocuous. They lack personal impact and engagement. Preaching leaves us bored and restless.

We tune out quickly when the preacher switches into his predictable routine. We have heard it all before, but we subdue a critical spirit, because, we say to ourselves, the sermon must

---

5. William H. Willimon, *Conversations with Barth on Preaching* (Nashville: Abingdon Press, 2006), p. 252.

be good for somebody. But who are we to assume that these bland sermons help the new believer or seeker? Even the preacher's affected tone and manner signals us to take refuge in our private thoughts. You have heard the story of the *Emperor's New Clothes*. Need I say more? The problem of *Canned Sermons* is the elephant in the room. Popular evangelical preachers seem to preach as *simply* as possibly and politically correct mainline Protestants seem to preach as *neutrally* as possible. Both camps set the bar low. The former is anti-intellectual and the latter is pseudointellectual.

The cultural captivity of the sermon is largely an undiagnosed problem. The apostle Paul warned that people will not put up with the whole counsel of God. Their itchy ears want a spiritual alternative to the truth.[6] However, the alternative is not, as we might have expected, an easily identifiable heresy. Instead, it is a subtle shift of emphasis away from the truth prompted by the audience's tastes. Preachers do not tickle the ears of their listeners with bold heretical notions, but with winsome common sense and humorous anecdotes. Paul might be surprised at how many preachers take their cue from standup comics and late night talk show hosts.

EVASION

A preacher in an upper-middle class church preached on Paul's prayer for the Philippians: "And this is my prayer: that your love may abound more and more in knowledge and depth of insight, so that you may be able to discern what is best and may be pure and blameless for the day of Christ."[7] His main

---

6. 2 Timothy 4:3.
7. Philippians 1:9-10.

emphasis was the advantage of acquiring a broad knowledge of life. "Ignorance is not bliss," he offered. "Whoever said, 'Ignorance is bliss,' got it wrong." He grew emphatic, "Tell me the advantages of not knowing math and science. Tell me the advantages of not knowing opera. There are none," he declared. "There are no advantages to not knowing." The preacher's stress on knowledge fit with his well-educated church.

So far so good, but it was what the preacher left out that was more telling than what he said. He carefully avoided any specific knowledge or insight that might contradict the wisdom of the world. He remained on a generic and abstract level of knowledge that caused no tension with the prevailing intellectual culture. Without exception, everyone, whether they believed in the Bible or not, could agree that we ought to expand our minds and embrace common sense. Yet the apostle Paul's concern was that this depth of insight and discernment help believers become "pure and blameless for the day of Christ." The preacher said nothing about the moral, ethical, and spiritual difference between the wisdom of the world and the wisdom of Christ. His intentional avoidance of any offense was provocative, especially for knowledgeable Christians who struggle with the conflict between the way of the world and obedience to God. The preacher's omission raised the issue of integrity.

An African-American preacher preached on Genesis 18, the appearance of the Lord to Abraham near the great trees of Mamre. He entitled his sermon, "Angels in the Neighborhood," and focused his theme on Abraham's response to the three visitors. The ancient patriarch "bowed low to the ground." The preacher used numerous illustrations drawn from the martial arts and the customs of other cultures to show how bowing shows respect. He led the congregation in practice bows and used the passage to teach about humility and dignity. His big idea was that we should always show respect because we never know when angels may be in the neighborhood. Missing entirely from the sermon was the meaning of why Yahweh met with Abraham and the importance of this encounter in salvation history. The preacher was animated and entertaining and the congregation loved it, but could we say that the gospel was preached that morning?

Whenever Jesus opened his mouth, he seemed to be offending someone, but thousands listen to preaching today that causes no offense. Jesus defended his ministry to John the Baptist, saying, "Blessed is the one who is not offended by me."[8] He offended his family, his hometown, the Pharisees, and the disciples. However, he went out of his way *not* to offend tax collectors. When Peter was offended over his Master's insistence on the cross, Jesus was offended by him.[9] Jesus was never rude or ugly in his comments. The offense arose because he tackled the tension between truth and disobedience—between truth and unbelief. His message was never in the abstract. He never engaged the scribal debate as if he were pressing for conceptual agreement on a propositional point. His preaching was always about transformation. He called men and women to leave their self-directed, self-righteous lives and take up their cross and follow him.

Every fall preachers preach on stewardship. In some churches the sermon series on giving is more important than preaching through Advent or Lent. My impression, having recently

---

8. Matthew 11:6
9. Matthew 13:57; 15:12; 17:27; 16:23

listened to a number of pastors on the subject of giving, was that the only offense of the gospel most pastors worry about is the one found in the stewardship sermon. Every pastor I heard began with either an apology for preaching on the subject or an explanation for why he wasn't giving an apology. It was difficult to resist the conclusion that *religiously* understood, "Stewardship" is when a greedy church makes greedy Christians feel guilty, so the church can profit from their greed and guilt. That sounds terribly cynical, but the line occurred to me when I was sitting in a beautiful three thousand seat, hi-tech sanctuary, equipped with huge video screens and a state-of-the art sound system, situated on a multimillion dollar church campus, and the pastor was preaching from the prophet Haggai. The pastor avoided leveling any materialistic indictment against the congregation. He assured the people that the Lord wanted them to prosper and to enjoy the good life. "Success," he assured them, "can be a sign of God's blessing." However, he felt compelled to inform them that their church was in ruins, yes, that's right in ruins, just like the house of God in Haggai's day, because they were three hundred thousand dollars behind in the general operating budget. "In a manner of speaking," he said, "you could say we too are in ruins!" No one gasped at this description. But they should have.

Søren Kierkegaard lamented that Christianity without Christ sought "to accomplish a great deal in the world, and to win great multitudes who desire also to be Christians only up to a certain point."[10] The possibility of offense was to be avoided at all cost. The purpose of Christianity was not to become like

---

10. Søren Kierkegaard, *Training in Christianity* (Princeton: Princeton University Press, 1957), pp. 108-109.

Jesus but to gain the approval and esteem of others. Self-respect rather than self-denial was the motivation for Christianity without Christ. Kierkegaard claimed that avoiding the offense was "out of hypocrisy or out of whimpering human sympathy for yourself or others." He concluded that preaching perpetually emphasized success and triumph: "in short, one hears only sermons, which might properly end with Hurrah! rather than with Amen." Becoming a Christian, complained Kierkegaard, meant joining a parade, not taking up a cross.

FAULT LINES

So then, what is this tension in the text, that we seem so good at avoiding? To summarize, the fault lines lie . . .

between God's salvation history and our personal story,

between biblical genres and our familiar styles of communication,

between the author's intended tension in the text, along with the canonical meaning of the passage, and our expectation of felt-need satisfaction,

between the truth that stands over and against us and our subjective selves seeking affirmation and approval,

between Jesus—living and Incarnate and innocuous Jesus talk.

Everyone has a story, but only one story redeems our story. Therein lies our first tension. As long as the preacher and the hearer stay in the small worlds of their own individual stories, they can avoid the tension, but as soon as they place their story in the context of God's Salvation History they are invited into the large world of God's making, redeeming, and reconciling. Too much of our preaching stays within the confines of our little worlds because the sermonic scope is limited to our immediate felt needs. But there are other fault lines.

The biblical genres—the way the Bible communicates—leads us into this tension. If the Bible came to us as lists and lectures, we might have an excuse for neglecting the overarching Gospel story, but instead it comes to us as historical narrative, wisdom literature, prophetic poetry, God-centered praise and lament, missional epistles, and historical apocalyptic. The Gospel accounts fuse and fulfill these genres. We are drawn into the tension between the Word of God and the way of the world. We wrestle with sin and salvation, judgment and worship, law and grace. Jesus' sermons are the furthest thing you can imagine from today's info-sermon and Christianized self-help. His parables thrive on twists and turns, exposing the fault lines that run between conventional thinking and the Gospel.

If the Bible used myth and fantasy, Schleiermacher's definition of preaching as "self-display with a stimulating effect" would make sense, but it doesn't. If we take the Bible seriously, and not as some kind of moralistic manual or Christian Qur'an, then we cannot help but be drawn into this Salvation Story—the truest of true stories. Our thinking is upended. Our sinful preoccupation with self is confronted. Our religious self-justification is challenged. We are not listing doctrines. We are engaged in a life of discipleship, living for Christ and his kingdom.

The tension in the text leads to the passion of the passage. We have to be careful not to truncate the text and edit out the tension. Many sermons miss the tension, because they skip over what the text is all about. Preachers select what they want to bring out from the text and ignore the context. They feel free to isolate a verse or lift out a line as a springboard into a sermon. They neglect the original tension in the text and preach a positive sermon on how to be a better Christian. They are preaching from the Bible but they ignore the tension that is there in the text between merit and mercy, judgment and salvation, the putting off and the putting on, sin and grace, idolatry and worship. Conventional sermons tell a clever opening story, plow through a text, make a few points and draw a conclusion, but in the process miss the passion of the passage. We have fallen into the bad habit of reading small portions of the Bible subjectively. Our focus is not on what the text means, but on a more self-centered question, "What does the text mean to me." Preachers have become more like Van Gogh than Rembrandt, they paint what they feel, not what they see. Our subjective experience trumps the tension in the text. After reading the Bible for a few minutes, whatever comes to mind becomes our devotional thought for the day. This practice may not be very different from praying the rosary. Surely, God can use these few minutes of Bible reading in the life of a believer, but it is not the best way to read the Bible.

Truncating the text can be a problem for those who take the text seriously. I recently heard a sermon on Paul's word of affirmation to the church at Philippi: "For it has been granted to you on behalf of Christ not only to believe on him, but also to suffer for him . . . "[11] The preacher spent forty minutes listing six or seven reasons why Christians benefit from suffering. He referenced texts from all over Scripture to make his points. His tone was that of a scholar listing points instead of a pastor encouraging people who are suffering. The preacher might just as well have been lecturing on the benefits of regular physical

---

11. Philippians 1:29

checkups. He never referred to the poignant tension between belief and suffering. He never asked the congregation if their belief in Christ had been tested by their suffering for Christ. The apostle Paul emphasized the privilege, "For it has been granted to you . . . " but the preacher focused more on information about suffering than comfort for those who were suffering.

He addressed his upper-middle class congregation, worshiping in their new 14 million dollar sanctuary, as if suffering were a potential problem that he wanted them prepared for in the future. But there must have been at least a few believers in such a large congregation who were experiencing the crucible of suffering. What if they had been lifted up as examples to us of those who were granted the privilege of going beyond belief to suffering? I thought of this because I was sitting next to a man who had suffered long and hard on the mission field and now his wife lay dying at home. I wondered how he was receiving this exposition on biblical suffering.

Instead of the text calling the shots and laying down its terms, many preachers believe that the text can be preached a thousand different ways. They can subjectively encounter any given biblical text and produce a so-called powerful sermon. Yes, indeed, they can sermonize any way they want, but the sermon will not be a biblical sermon even though it allegedly comes out of the Bible. If *our* context controls the text then *we* are the text, not the Bible. Much of our devotional and sermonic material fails to identify the tension in the text and thus fails to grasp the true passion of the passage.

Preaching has been defined as truth through personality. That is to say, the tension in the text runs right through the pastor. If that tension does not resonate with the preacher, so that the preacher is disturbed and delighted, comforted and challenged, then the preacher is not ready to preach. If the preacher hasn't experienced the passion of the passage, doesn't feel the dissonance between the Word of God and the human condition, then chances are the congregation won't experience it either. It is important not to confuse the tension in the text with self-doubt and anxiety. The tension is derived from the text, the message intended by the original author, and not the psychological angst of the preacher. All too often, we miss the most obvious sense of the text and bring our own agendas instead.

Poor preaching can be used mightily by the Spirit of Christ to preach the Gospel and make disciples. It happens every Sunday morning, but that's no excuse for poor preaching. Thankfully, "God in his ordinary providence makes use of means, yet is free to work without, above and against them, at his pleasure" —and for his glory![12] How much better when the preacher is standing on the fault line between the mystery of God and the mess of the human condition and preaches the Word as it was intended to be preached. Good preaching requires discernment and hard work. It doesn't take a genius. It takes someone who will pay attention prayerfully and thoughtfully to God's overarching salvation history, the original intention of the passage, the context of the text, and the people to whom one is preaching.

A faithful pastor preached on "Loving Service" from John 13. The sermon was part of a series he preached to help define the household of faith as a worshiping, learning, loving and serving body of believers. Knowing this pastor as I do, I am confident that a great deal of prayer and study went into the selection of the text and the preparation of the message. He did a fine job

---

12. Westminster Confession, on Providence, V, 3.

presenting the necessity of foot washing for a group of men walking the dusty, dirty roads of Palestine in the first century. He emphasized the awkwardness around the table as none of the disciples deemed it their responsibility to take on the role of a servant and wash the disciples' feet. No one was willing to humble themselves even though it was a breech of etiquette to recline at the low table with unwashed feet.

He noted that Jesus' loving service issued out of his fullness. Jesus didn't need to be needed. There was nothing lacking in his life that needed to be fulfilled by giving himself away to others. To illustrate this he said, "It is like the popular high school senior who goes out of her way to reach out to an unpopular girl." But then he added as an aside, "I can't say that of a junior higher, because if a popular junior higher reached out to an unpopular student, she would immediately become unpopular." His little aside, which I'm not even sure he intended to say, unwittingly backed into the tension in the text. He wanted to use the text to illustrate humble service in the church. This is the obvious truth that everyone gets on a quick read of the passage and this is where the illustration of the popular student who lowers herself to reach out to others fits the theme. But John designed the text to go deeper. John wants us to see the tension between Peter and Judas in how they react to Jesus' humility.

John sets up the dramatic foot-washing scene with a fourfold emphasis on the immediacy of Jesus' death. He sets the scene in the context of salvation history. This is much more than a story about service. First, he speaks of the Passover knowing that Jesus is the Passover Lamb who takes away the sin of the world. Second, he refers to the hour. Jesus is aware "that the hour had come for him to leave this world and go to the Father."

Third, what is to follow is a sign of how Jesus loved his disciples "to the end." From foot-washing to the cross is in John's mind a full picture of how Jesus loved and served the disciples. Fourth, John explains the role that Judas will play in betraying Jesus.

John makes foot-washing and going to the cross one continuous expression of Jesus' love for his own. The tension in the text builds as Peter and Judas are seen as contrasting pictures of acceptance and rejection. At first Peter resisted Jesus' initiative, but when he understands that foot-washing is a picture of a necessary and deep inner-life cleansing, that only Jesus in his fullness and in his love can perform, he is enthusiastic ("Not just my feet, Lord, but my whole body!"). Judas, on the other hand, despises Jesus for stripping down and becoming a servant. Judas is like the junior higher in the preacher's analogy. He can't handle the humility of Jesus without being humiliated.

There is a difference between presenting this text as a lesson in loving service and discovering in it the tension between God's sacrificial love and our willingness to receive his grace. The passion of the passage defines love's full extent in terms of the cross of Christ. Practical lessons on how to serve one another are important, but they are best framed by the humility and grace of the crucified Lord. Everything about this scene points to the cross. The passion of the passage is not about what we can do for God, but what God in Christ has done for us.

6

TEXT SAVVY

If we are going to let the Word of God dwell in us the way Jesus, the Living Word, dwelled among us, then we have to reexamine the way we preach the text. We have to read it and preach it in the light of the pedagogical impact and communicational model of the Incarnation. Otherwise, we may be missing out on something important. The paradigm for all Christian communication is the Incarnate One: Truth in Person, absolute truth embodied, independent of all contingencies, spoken into the personal, earthy contingencies of daily life. "The Word was made flesh and dwelt among us and we beheld his glory, the glory of the only begotten full of grace and truth."[1] God, in the flesh, bears witness in our mundane world. The most real world interfaces with our all-too-real-world. The Incarnate One moves into our neighborhood. There is nothing abstract and theoretical about this. Belief is not a cognitive assent to ideas, but a living relationship of obedience, a daily following after Jesus, our crucified and risen Lord. We don't become Jesus,

---

1. John 1:14.

but we become like Jesus as the Spirit of Christ indwells us. The Word in-bodied defines us as we follow the Incarnate Word.

SELF-EMPTYING

Self-emptying is the key. Meekness is the *modus operandi*. God transcended his own being by becoming human. He emptied himself of himself, his divine attributes and prerogatives, and became obedient to death—even death on a cross! This lowliness produces the contradiction that the truth of the Gospel must suffer in a world that makes success and self-achievement into a god that fashions immortality symbols out of children and houses and adventures. The Creator became a creature. The followers of Jesus are to become like Jesus, unrecognizable by the world, incognito, bearing the truth essential for the world's salvation, all the while living under the radar. For the sake of Christ and His Kingdom all worldly triumphalism must be forsaken. The tension in the text is made possible by the Author of life who intervened in the Story he spoke into existence. Meekness is a fitting description of the living God who reveals himself slowly, personally and with great reserve. The climax of God's great salvation history is reached in the Incarnation at the point of God's greatest humility and vulnerability, but the clarity and the victory of God's redemptive love are never in doubt. Inherent in this entire history is the meekness of God that seeks to love and forgive us.

Emily Dickinson's poetic line, "Tell all the Truth but tell it slant," underscores the need to get at the truth in ways that serve the truth, rather than stifle it. If the Incarnate One is the Way, the Truth, and the Life, and the single most important paradigm for all Christian communication, then doesn't that tell us something about how we should communicate the truth of God's Word? And this applies, not just in sermons, but in casual conversation, table talk, and lectures. We experience too much religious verbiage and sanctimonious talk in church and a psychological censorship of the truth almost everywhere else. Kierkegaard contended that the truth of the God-Man eliminated all direct communication, making it impossible to turn the wisdom of Christianity into cognitive formulas that people only needed to agree to in order to become believers. Instead of agreeing to a few bullet points, we have to honestly, humbly, radically follow Jesus! We have to listen to him. Kierkegaard lamented the pervasive influence of Christendom on preaching. He wrote,

> One might well weep at the state that Christianity has been reduced to in Christendom, considering what the pastors in their sermons again and again repeat, with the utmost assurance, as if they were saying something most striking and convincing. What they say is that Christ directly affirmed that he was God, the Only Begotten of the Father; they are horrified at any suggestion of concealment, as a thing unworthy of Christ, as vain trifling with regard to a serious matter, the most serious matter of all, the salvation of man. Ah, such parsons do not know what they are talking about, it is hidden from their eyes that they are doing away with Christianity. . . .Direct recognizableness is precisely the characteristic of the pagan god.
> . . .Take away the possibility of offense, as they have done in Christendom, and the whole of Christianity is direct communication; and then Christianity is done away with, for it has become an easy thing, a superficial something which neither wounds nor heals profoundly enough; it is the false invention of human sympathy which forgets the infinite qualitative difference between God and man.[2]

---

2. Søren Kierkegaard, *Training in Christianity*, pp. 134, 139.

Christianity without Christ seems to echo Jesus' unbeliev-
ing brothers in John 7. As the Feast of Tabernacles approached,
they chided Jesus, saying, "No one who wants to become a
public figure acts in secret. Since you are doing these things,
show yourself to the world." As if to say, "If you want people
to believe in you, you have to work for it. You have to run for
office. You have to lay out your agenda and make your case." It
was obvious to them that Jesus had chosen a radically different
method of communication, one that in their opinion was bound
to fail. Dependent upon the Father's timing and teaching,
Jesus didn't make a move or open his mouth without raising
questions and leaving confusion. His proclamation of the truth
was provocative. He caused people to think, challenging their
assumptions and exposing their prejudices. Some even used his
perception against him, accusing him of being paranoid ("You
are demon-possessed. Who is trying to kill you?").

The crowd at the Feast was divided over Jesus. Some
thought he was a deceiver, others thought he was a prophet,
and still others that he was the Messiah. For some he was too
well known ("But we know where this man is from; when the
Messiah comes, no one will know where he is from."). Their
Bible knowledge got in the way of their belief. They were hung
up on the fact that Jesus was from Galilee. The Pharisees kept
their distance. They could hear the whispers of the crowd, but
they couldn't hear Jesus.[3] Yet with all this confusion and chaos
generated by unbelief and resistance, Jesus didn't bullet point
his message. He refused to clear up the confusion and reduce
his message to a list of explicit propositions. He kept coming at
the truth paradoxically. "You know me," he says, "but you don't

---

3.   John 7:39

know the one who sent me . . . You will look for me, but you will not find me." He even spoke of the Spirit filling believers with rivers of living water, but the Spirit had not been given yet. Of all the people listening to Jesus or trying not to listen to Jesus, the guards sum it up best, "No one ever spoke the way this man does." The Jesus way of communicating needs to impress us more, so that when people hear us preaching the gospel they think of Jesus.

TRUTH TOLD SLANT

The blunt and boring explicitness of today's sermons, laying it all out in bullet points, and sound bites with movie clips, is ruining people's minds for the very truth we seek to commend to them. We have confused the truth of Christ with ways of communicating that are better suited to the marketplace and campaign trail. Proclamation borders on propaganda. The pulpiteer has become a puppeteer, massaging and manipulating, pulling the strings on unwitting parishioners. Corporations now hire people they call "evangelists" to sell their product and famous preachers are under lucrative corporate contracts to motivate executives. When will we wake up and see just how bad off we really are? Not soon enough.

Truth told slant lies behind the evident lack of explanation for the Atonement. Publicity would have been completely inconsistent with the preparations that had been made for the Atonement throughout salvation history by means of illustrations, types, and the sacrificial system. God in his meekness has always allowed his actions to speak louder than his words. He did not give Cain and Abel a theology lesson before choosing Abel's sacrifice and disqualifying Cain's. He did not carefully explain to Abraham how the command to sacrifice his son

Isaac was a picture of the will of the Father in giving up his one and only Son. Nor did God explain to Job that he would take a world of unjust suffering and nail it to the cross. He let King David and the prophets discover that a broken and contrite heart meant more than sacrifices.

It would be foolish to conclude from the lack of publicity and the absence of pedantic instruction about the Cross in the Gospels that the meaning of the Cross is somehow disqualified for lack of information and doctrinal explanation. Later, the Epistles will explain and expound on the wonder of the Atonement, but it is helpful to contemplate the reasons for this initial reserve. First of all, there is more going on within the relationships of the triune God than we could begin to imagine, much less figure out and reduce to bullet points. P. T. Forsyth wisely observes:

> Christ came not to say something, but to do something. His revelation was more action than instruction. He revealed by redeeming. The thing He did was not simply to make us aware of God's disposition in an impressive way. It was not to *declare* forgiveness. It was certainly not to *explain* forgiveness. And it was not even to bestow forgiveness. It was to *effect* forgiveness, to set up the relation of forgiveness both in God and man. . . . The great mass of Christ's work was like a stable iceberg. It was hidden. It was His dealing with God, not man. The great thing was done with God. It was independent of our knowledge of it. The greatest thing ever done in the world was done out of sight. The most ever done for us was done behind our backs. Only it was we who had turned our backs. Doing this for us was the first condition of doing anything with us.[4]

---

4. P. T. Forsyth, *God: The Holy Father* (Blackwood, South Australia: New Creation Publications, 1987), pp.13-14.

The meekness of God is revealed in the Father's reserve, and in the Son's reticence, and in the Spirit's selflessness. Divine meekness has no parallel in the history of man-made gods and in the religions of human origin and invention. And it is essential that we realize that this meekness is not for show, but is inherent in the will of God and in the internal communion of the Father, Son and Holy Spirit. It is the meekness of the Father that wills to redeem humankind through love and grace. It is the meekness of the Son that proves the Father's will and preserves the integrity of the Incarnation. And it is the meekness of the Spirit who was sent not to speak on his own behalf, but to bear witness to Jesus Christ.[5] If the triune God chose to reveal, redeem and sanctify us in this way, we ought to embrace meekness as the way of life most consistent with following Christ.

Telling the truth slant, the way Jesus did, meets two important communicational needs: first, it gets past the listener's defenses and second, it does so without diminishing the listener. Text savvy preachers value the truth and respect the listener. Those who would "throw pearls to pigs" to fulfill their self-imposed religious obligations feel relieved that they have gotten the gospel out. But the gospel they are selling bears faint resemblance to the biblical gospel. They see their job as getting people to accept Jesus, but the Jesus they showcase is nothing like the real Jesus. They want people to sign on the dotted line, but Jesus wants them to take up their cross and follow him. They make admirers of Jesus and Jesus wants followers. The blunt force of today's simplistic consumer gospel subjects the biblical gospel to frivolous and unnecessary contempt. It may

5.   John 16:13-15

attract many, but it repels many more. Dietrich Bonhoeffer wrote,

> Every attempt to impose the gospel by force, to run after people and proselytize them, to use our own resources to arrange salvation for other people, is both futile and dangerous. It is futile, because the swine do not recognize the pearls that are cast before them, and dangerous, because it profanes the word of forgiveness, by causing those we fain would serve to sin against that which is holy.[6]

Educator Parker Palmer likens the soul to a wild animal, "tough, resilient, and yet shy." We have to approach the soul with care. We cannot confront the soul head-on and get very far. A startled soul escapes for its life. "When we go crashing through the woods shouting for it to come out so we can help it, the soul will stay in hiding."[7] But if we are willing to follow Jesus' strategy of incarnation and meekness, we will carry on a real conversation with people that gets past their defenses and cares for their soul.

Palmer observes that "people do not willingly return to a conversation that diminishes them."[8] Sometimes I am not so sure, because bad preaching seems to have a strange way of defying the odds and building a popular following. People may be drawn to poor preaching for any number of reasons, but that doesn't change the fact that those who aim to preach prophetically seek to engage the listener as a thinking human being who deserves all the respect and care we would give to a close

---

6. Dietrich Bonhoeffer, *The Cost of Discipleship* (New York: Macmillan, 1963), p. 206.

7. Parker Palmer, *The Courage to Teach: Exploring The Inner Landscape of a Teacher's Life* (San Francisco: Jossey-Bass, 1998), p. 151

8. Parker Palmer, p. 145.

friend. Good preaching doesn't play to the crowd, manipulate the emotions, or override the brain. Nor does it waste people's time. It refuses to dumb-down the Gospel and shrink-wrap the whole counsel of God into some quick snack that can be eaten on the run.

Good preaching is practical without being pragmatic and moving without being sensational. If the message is boring and repetitive to the preacher, chances are it is boring and repetitive to the listener. Preaching is a labor of love that demands great insight, intense prayer, and behind-the-scenes energy. All good preachers seek to point people to Christ, not themselves. Instead of basking in the lime light they want to shine the light on Jesus. Good preachers cultivate a humility that causes them to resist being the center of attention. There is a sense of urgency and immediacy in good preaching that defies the flippant and casual air of today's seriously unserious culture. Preachers extend themselves as Jesus would. They issue a loving appeal, a call to reason, a desire for dialogue. They echo the prophet Isaiah, when he said, "'Come now, let us reason together,' says the Lord. 'Though your sins are like scarlet, they will be as white as snow; though they are red as crimson, they will be like wool'"[9]. Like Jesus, good preachers proclaim without the presumption of agreement and the cockiness of success. In short, they refuse to diminish their listeners.

Text savvy preaching inevitably finds its way to the Cross. The apostle Paul said, "For I resolved to know nothing while I was with you except Jesus Christ and him crucified."[10] He saw the relevance of the Cross in every conceivable sphere

---

9.   Isaiah 1:18
10. 1 Corinthians 2:2

of the believer's life. He saw the Cross of Jesus as the basis for unity in the Body of Christ. To those who were ready to divide up and follow their favorite leader he asked, "Was Paul crucified for you? Were you baptized into the name of Paul?"[11] To those who were proud of their tolerance of sexual immorality in the church, Paul called for immediate church discipline because, "Christ our Passover lamb has been sacrificed."[12] He commanded, "Flee from sexual immorality," because of the Cross. "You are not your own, you were bought at a price. Therefore honor God with your body."[13] He counseled believers to experience their freedom in Christ, regardless of their social circumstances, because of the Cross. "You were bought at a price; do not become slaves of men."[14] He advised refraining from eating meat that had been offered to idols if it would cause a new believer to stumble. Or else, " . . . this weak brother, for whom Christ died, is destroyed by your knowledge."[15]

Paul centered the worship life of the church in the Cross. "Is not the cup of thanksgiving for which we give thanks a participation in the blood of Christ? And is not the bread that we break a participation in the body of Christ?"[16] He warned believers against using their social positions and income to humiliate other believers. "For anyone who eats and drinks without recognizing the body of the Lord eats and drinks judgment on himself."[17] To those who questioned the reality of

---

11. 1 Cor 1:13
12. 1 Cor 5:7
13. 1 Cor 6:19-20
14. 1 Cor 7:23
15. 1 Cor 8:11
16. 1 Cor 10:16
17. 1 Cor 11:29

the bodily resurrection, Paul affirmed that the saving work of Christ on the cross depended upon the risen Lord Jesus. "For what I received I passed on to you as of the first importance: that Christ died for our sins according to the Scriptures, that he was buried, that he was raised on the third day according to the Scriptures, and that he appeared to Peter, and then to the Twelve."[18]

In the midst of every problem, every issue, every conflict impacting the church at Corinth, Paul brought the believers back to the finished work of Christ on the Cross. Paul subsumed everything under the cross, even death itself. "The sting of death is sin, and the power of sin is the law. But thanks be to God! He gives us the victory through our Lord Jesus Christ."[19] Text savvy preaching is always heading to the Cross and preaching Resurrection hope.

---

18. 1 Cor 15:3-4
19. 1 Cor 15:56

7

TEXTING JESUS' STYLE

Kayla recently graduated from Vanderbilt University. She grew up in northern Alabama and attended church all of her life. Her minister back home preached three sermons no matter what Scripture passage he chose: God loves you and you need to accept Jesus; God loves you and you need to come to church; God loves you and if you don't love him back, you're going to hell. Guilt was the nagging motivator in her mentally challenged sub-cultural Christianity. In her senior year of high-school, her mother had an affair and her parents divorced. She went to live with her father. Kayla was in emotional pain from her parents' divorce, as well as getting over an abusive relationship, when she joined the Baptist fellowship at Vanderbilt. For the first time she met thoughtful Christians— believers devoted to Jesus Christ as Lord. This opened up a whole new world for her. For the first time she discovered what it meant to follow the Lord Jesus. Kayla realized that she, along with all Christians, was called to salvation, service, sacrifice and simplicity. This transformed her life. She sought to love the Lord her God with her whole being and her neighbor as herself.

Kayla had to wait until college to discover the power and depth of the Word of God. She suffered spiritual malpractice at the hands of a minister who abused the text and distorted the Christian life. Her minister had never been to seminary, but the solution to poor preaching is not attending seminary. We don't have to go to seminary to learn to preach well, and graduating from seminary is no assurance that we will preach well, but we do have to pay attention to Jesus. That's the key, learning to handle the text the way Jesus did; proclaiming the Truth the way Jesus did.

LISTEN TO JESUS

In the Gospel of Matthew, Jesus began his public preaching ministry with the Sermon on the Mount and ended it with the Sermon on the End of the World.[1] These two sermons frame his teaching ministry and offer insights into Jesus the Preacher. They model for the church how preachers should preach. If we want to learn how to preach, we need to pay attention to Jesus. Most of us are more familiar with the Sermon on the Mount than we are with the Sermon on the End of the World, but even then few of us understand Jesus' twelve minute Sermon on the Mount as a whole. Preachers tend to break it up and preach it piecemeal. We have been taught to dissect Matthew 5-7 into small sections for microscopic exegetical examination or for homiletical sound bites. Instead of grasping the totality of the sermon, we think of the sermon as a collection of random sayings and reflections from Jesus. Then, we turn to textual technicians to decipher and decode the text. Preaching, however, is neither solving an intellectual puzzle nor appealing

---

1. Matthew 5-7; 24-25

to an audience's emotional felt needs. Preaching is proclaiming the whole counsel of God in the Jesus way.

The Sermon on the Mount begins with a three-fold emphasis: beatitude based spiritual formation, salt and light ministry impact, and the fulfillment of the Law through heart righteousness. Jesus goes on to contrast his teaching with conventional thinking ("You have heard it said ... but I say to you"). He describes the visible righteousness the world was meant to see: love instead of hate, purity instead of lust, fidelity instead of infidelity, honesty instead of dishonesty, reconciliation instead of retaliation, and prayer instead of revenge. This is followed by the hidden righteousness of giving, praying and fasting which is for our Heavenly Father's eyes only. Five "do nots" mark the boundaries of true freedom: do not give your heart to material things; do not make money your master; do not worry about material things; do not judge others harshly; and do not force the gospel on others. Then, pray—ask, seek, knock, and your heavenly Father will give whatever you need to do for others what you would have them do to you. The conclusion of the sermon is a warning: choose the narrow gate, not Broadway; watch out for false teachers; produce good fruit, not bad; beware! pious words are no substitute for obedience; make sure you build on the foundation that will not give way in the storms of life.

Modern sermons have a way of easing us out the door into the virtual reality of business as usual. But Jesus' sermons never worked that way, and they still don't. Dire consequences await those who do not heed these warnings. This is how Jesus began his preaching ministry: working from the inside out; resting on the Word of God; embracing the totality of the believer's life— theologically, ethically, and spiritually; clarifying values, vision and loyalties; and ending the sermon decisively. Jesus concludes the Sermon on the Mount on a negative note. "Everyone who hears these words of mine and puts them into practice is blessed, but the one who doesn't crashes. Amen." It's over. Time to go. He gets up to leave. It won't work to say, "Good sermon, Jesus, see you next week."

We are impressed. Jesus is not homiletical in the traditional sense. He is not an actor on a stage or a politician on the stump or a king holding court or a professor at the lectern, and he certainly is not a preacher with PowerPoint. He is the Teacher in conversation with his disciples. He is at eye level, meeting us face to face, heart to heart. We're not tricked into watching him on some 12' by 12' video screen. Against every high-strung emotion and attention-deficit disorder impulse, he calls us to listen. His words are not bubble speech filling the space over an animated preacher delivering clever one liners.

We are inundated with all kinds of rhetoric: ESPN's passionate intensity; Joel Osteen's gospel of health and wealth; Comedy Central's cynicism on the day's news; Fox News' incessant doomsday harangue, and First Church's innocuous speech. Enough. Shut up. Jesus is speaking. His straight forward intensity recalls the prophets. His theology is steeped in the Old Testament. His method of communication is analogical, not anecdotal; authoritative, not authoritarian; penetrating, not pedantic. Jesus loves earthy metaphors and down-to-earth obedience. Form follows function. Jesus isn't sermonizing, delivering religious talks to make nice people nicer. He is turning everything upside down, transforming life from top to bottom. People who take his Message to heart have a new beatitude-based identity, with salt and light impact—rooted in the Word of God. They hold to the grace-based Kingdom ethic and choose the Rock solid foundation.

THE LAST SERMON

Then, three years later and two days before his last Passover, Jesus gave his last sermon. Dale Bruner comments, "Jesus' Sermon on the End of the World is simply Jesus' Sermon on the Mount under pressure."[2] The occasion for the sermon was his leaving the temple for the last time; the setting of the sermon was the Mount of Olives. Jesus was hot—agitated, accusatory, fierce in tone and temper. He burned with anger against the teachers of the law and the Pharisees for their hypocrisy, showy piety, and hostility to the revelation of God. Like Isaiah, Jesus pronounced seven woes.[3] He called them names: "You hypocrites! You snakes! You brood of vipers! He blamed them for the blood of the prophets from the blood of righteous Abel to the blood of Zechariah. His parting words were, "For I tell you, you will not see me again until you say, 'Blessed is he who comes in the name of the Lord.'"[4]

I'm not sure how the disciples understood this blistering prophetic rebuke, because as Jesus was leaving the temple, "his disciples came up to him to call his attention to its buildings." That must have been about the last thing on Jesus' mind—the buildings. I wonder which one of the disciples made it a point of calling Jesus' attention to the buildings. It may have been a group effort or it may have been Peter. Remember it was Peter

---

2. Dale Bruner, *Matthew: A Commentary, vol. 2. The Churchbook, Matthew 13-18* (Grand Rapids, MI: Eerdmans, 2004), p. 488.

3. Isaiah 5:8-6:5

4. Matthew 23:39

who had wanted to construct three shelters on the Mount of Transfiguration. His big idea was interrupted by the voice of the Father saying, "This is my Son, whom I love; with him I am well pleased. Listen to him!"[5] How is it that we disciples are so easily distracted? Why do we stop listening to Jesus? Given what Jesus had just finished saying in the temple court who had the nerve to stop him and call attention to the temple buildings? If the disciples had a camera they would have asked Jesus to pose for a group photo.

The disciples were trying to get Jesus to notice "how the temple was adorned with beautiful stones and with gifts dedicated to God," but Luke reports that Jesus noticed the poor widow giving her offering of two very small copper coins. Jesus made an example of her. Her act of worship provided a teachable moment. "Truly I tell you," he said, "this poor widow has put in more than all the others. All these people gave their gifts out of their wealth; but she out of her poverty put in all she had to live on."[6]

Jesus concludes the Sermon on the End of the World with a description of the Last Judgment. He highlights the difference between the saved and the lost with a simple picture. The division between the saved and the lost, will be as simple as a shepherd dividing sheep and goats. And the telling characteristic of the saved is that they *see* invisible people like this poor widow and the lost don't. We need to keep this poor widow who gave her all in mind, because her story begins the sermon that Jesus will finish with the description of the Last Judgment.

---

5. Matthew 17:5
6. Luke 21:3-5

Following Pentecost, Peter and John were about to enter the temple, when a lame man asked them for money. Peter said to the man, "Look at us! Silver and gold I do not have, but what I do have I give you. In the name of Jesus Christ of Nazareth, walk!"[7] Luke reports, "He jumped to his feet and began to walk. Then he went with them into the temple courts, walking and jumping and praising God." People recognized that this was the lame man who had sat at the temple gate called Beautiful, and they were filled with wonder and amazement at what had happened to him. What could be more beautiful than the temple? What could be more amazing than the gate called Beautiful? The answer: A poor lame beggar on his feet walking, jumping and dancing—praising God. You know the story. Peter preached his second message after Pentecost and he and John were hauled before the Sanhedrin. Then, Peter, filled with the Holy Spirit said,

> It is by the name of Jesus Christ of Nazareth, whom you crucified but whom God raised from the dead, that this man stands before you healed. Jesus is the 'stone you builders rejected, which has become the cornerstone.' Salvation is found in no one else, for there is no other name given under heaven by which you must be saved.[8]

These two events converge: Jesus leaves the temple, praising the poor widow and preaching the Sermon on the End of the World; Peter and John are dragged from the temple, after healing the lame man, to stand trial before the Sanhedrin. Peter's Spirit filled message confirms that Jesus has replaced the temple. All the same factors are present: a beautiful temple

---

7. Acts 3:4-6
8. Acts 4:10-12

is eclipsed by the beauty of the gospel of Jesus Christ transforming needy people.

Zambian New Testament scholar Joe Kapolyo emphasizes the significance of Jesus turning his back on Judaism and abandoning the whole sacrificial system.[9] What Jesus refuses to do is turn his back on the Jewish people! The destruction of the temple prophesied in Jesus' Last Sermon signifies not only the end of Judaism but the end of all religions, including Christendom. Only Christ fulfills the human need for salvation and the longing of the soul. If the temple is done away with, how much more will all religious traditions be eclipsed by the presence of Jesus? Jesus is Lord. He is the one who is greater than Judaism, Islam, Hinduism, Confucianism, ancestral worship, and all forms of tribal animism and existential selfism.

Had not Jesus said? "I tell you that one greater than the temple is here."[10] I don't know which disciple tried to get his attention, but I know he must have regretted it, because Jesus sounds angry: "Do you see all these things? Truly I tell you, not one stone here will be left on another; every one will be thrown down." It is impossible to say these words wistfully with a hint of melancholy or regretfully with a tone of disappointment. These are fighting words and one wonders if they were not reported back to the Sanhedrin as treasonous words. Before the Sanhedrin, Jesus' false accusers will quote Jesus as saying, "We heard him say, 'I will destroy this temple made with human hands and in three days will build another, not made with hands.'"[11] Enough said. Jesus was heading to the Mount

---

9. Joe Kapolyo, "Matthew," *Africa Bible Commentary*, ed. Tokunboh Adeyemo, ed. (Grand Rapids, MI: Zondervan, 2006), p. 1161.

10. Matthew 12:6

11. Matthew 14:58

of Olives. From there he would look down on the temple and preach his last sermon.

SETTING THE SERMON

Good preachers do not force themselves on people. Jesus' pedagogical pattern takes advantage of the situation, but his method does not manipulate people. "As Jesus was sitting on the Mount of Olives, the disciples came to him privately." Even John the Baptist's voice of judgment in the wilderness was a sermon heard, not because of publicity and good marketing, but because people were drawn to the truth. "People went out to him from Jerusalem and all Judea and the whole region of the Jordan."[12] What Jesus said as he and his disciples were leaving the temple raised the question that prompted the sermon: "*When* will the temple be destroyed?" Unlike the Sermon on the Mount, the Sermon on the End of the World was preached to only the disciples. There was no surrounding crowd made up of the curious, the critical and the casual. What Jesus preached on the Mount of Olives was intended for the disciples, not the teachers of the law or the Pharisees. Only the disciples heard this sermon. This provocative, prophetic and poetic message was meant for them.

The disciples came to Jesus with a question. He did not impose his sermon on them. But Jesus didn't answer their question, at least not directly. Good preaching does not bow before our "felt need" questions or cater to our sense of relevancy. Good preaching shifts the focus from our questions to necessary truth. In this sermon, *Jesus dampens speculation on the end times and ramps up readiness for the end times*. The

---

12. Matthew 3:5

disciples want Jesus to say *when* all this will happen and Jesus wants to describe how *then* we should live. "Then" (tote) is one of Matthew's favorite words."[13] The focus is not so much on the timing of the end, but of being faithful to the end. The speculative curiosity of *when* is trumped by the sober consideration of *then*. "Then they will deliver you up to tribulation . . . ;" "And then many will fall away. . . ; "Who then is the faithful and wise servant. . .;" "Then the kingdom of heaven will be like ten virgins. . .[14] Given what has happened, is happening, and will happen how then should we live?

The *beginning of the end* began with the coming of Jesus, the Incarnate One, on Christmas Day in Bethlehem and the *end of the beginning* came when the temple was destroyed in 70 AD. The end of the beginning of the last days, starts when Jesus walked out of the temple and three days later the curtain of the temple was torn in two.[15] "The temple worship of the ancient people of God is all over and the way to God's holy presence has been opened up for all by means of this one sacrifice for the sin of the whole world."[16]

Ever since Jesus came we have been in the last days and these last days will not be over until Jesus returns. Between the miracle of his birth and the miracle of his return, the disciples "work out their salvation with fear and trembling."[17] Jesus prepares us for all types of trouble: spiritual deception, political upheaval, social disasters, persecution and tribulation. The focus of Jesus' Sermon on the End of the World is faithful-

---

13. Bruner, p. 483.
14. Matthew 24:9-10, 45; 25:1
15. Matthew 27:51
16. Bruner, p. 757
17. Philippians 2:12

ness to the end. It is all about discernment (not speculation), resilience (not escape), readiness (not passivity), obedience (not indifference), and ministry in the name of Jesus. His message has two themes woven together: no-fear-apocalyptic and fear-of-the-Lord parabolic.

NO-FEAR APOCALYPTIC

Jesus tells the story of the consummation of the age "in the prophetic style in which two or more events are viewed simultaneously through the same lens."[18] Near at hand, and within the first generation of believers, is the destruction of the temple. In the distance, at a day or hour no one knows, is the coming of the Son of Man. All disciples live between these two events. We live between *the already and the not yet*, between random acts of historical violence and the perseverance of the saints, between the normality of eating and drinking, marrying and giving in marriage and the immediacy of Christ's return, between the world's hate producing apostasy and the church's mission of God heralding the gospel throughout the world. We live between the coming of the Son of Man that no one can miss, because it's like lightning flashing from east to west and the final coming of the Son of Man when we least expect it. Ministry happens today, not sometime in the future. Testing, trials, and tribulations are not off in the future, they are now.

Jesus preached a complex sermon with truth-slanting simplicity. He fused complex salvation history and simple story and created a tension in the text between no-fear apocalyptic and fear-of-the-Lord parabolic. Trust in the midst of deception, chaos and apostasy, is held in tension with straight-forward

18. Kapoloyo, p. 1161

obedience. If we have ears to hear we can understand his message but we can never exhaust his message.

The complexity of the sermon can be attributed to how Jesus drew on his Old Testament sources: Daniel's abomination that causes desolation; Isaiah's description of the day of the Lord; Zechariah's mourned and martyred messiah; and Noah's evil age of complacency before the cataclysm. The complexity of the sermon can also be found in how Jesus developed the scope and the sequence of salvation history. Jesus unfurls a picture of the end that is all encompassing. His scope could not be greater: "nation will arise against nation," "the gospel of the kingdom will be preached in the whole world as a testimony to all the nations," angels will "gather his elect from the four winds, from one end of the heavens to the other," "all the peoples of the earth will mourn," and "all the nations will be gathered before him, and he will separate the people from one another as a shepherd separates the sheep from the goats." The most obvious complexity of the sermon lies in the sequence of events. Jesus merges immediacy and longevity into a single stream of urgency. The sermon causes us to see events as God sees them, in the present tense.

Added to the complexity of this message, is the intensity of Jesus' Last Sermon. There is nothing laid back about Jesus' message, both the complexity and the intensity contradict our conventional sermonizing. From his opening, "Watch out," to his closing, "Then they will go away to eternal punishment, but the righteous to eternal life," everything is extreme. The coming of the Son of Man is like lightning, the sun will be darkened and the stars will fall from the sky.

Extremism invades his parables. The fate of the wicked household servant is gruesome: ". . .cut him to pieces and assign him a place with the hypocrites, where there will be weeping and gnashing of teeth." The useless servant in the parable of the talents is thrown outside, "into the darkness, where there will be weeping and gnashing of teeth." In the description of the Last Judgment, the apathetic, the indifferent, the clueless, the unresponsive, and the selfish, will be told, "Depart from me, you who are cursed, into the eternal fire prepared for the devil and his angels."

Jesus' sermon is filled with concern for his disciples that they not fall away, because of deception, wars, famines, earthquakes, persecutions, apostasy, and the destruction of the temple.

Concern number one: Deception. Christians are in danger of deception from tricksters who claim to be little messiahs or special representatives of Christ. These deceivers are not broadcasting, "I am the messiah," nor impersonating Jesus, but they are drawing attention to themselves and claiming to fulfill the role and title that belong to Jesus. Jesus warns us that this is not a rare phenomenon. There will be *many* super-Christians who will deceive *many* by pointing to themselves. These heroic Christians remind us of the *many* referred to in the Sermon on the Mount: "*Many* will say to me on that day, 'Lord, Lord, did we not prophesy in your name and in your name drive out demons and in your name perform many miracles?' Then I will tell them plainly, 'I never knew you. Away from me, you evildoers!'"[19] Jesus' number one concern and the greatest danger facing Christians comes from within Christendom. Professing Christians pose the greatest threat. *Don't be deceived. Keep your theological sanity.*[20]

---

19. Matthew 7:22-23
20. Bruner, p. 482

Concern number two: Fear. There will be social upheaval: wars, famines, earthquakes, family break-ups, financial meltdowns, epidemics, and social and political problems of all kinds. "Such things must happen, but the end is still to come." Cycles of upheaval, centuries of pain and plague and political chaos, will be routine. "All these are the beginning of birth pains," wrote the apostle Paul. "For the creation was subjected to frustration, not by its own choice, but by the will of the one who subjected it, in hope that the creation itself will be liberated from its bondage to decay and brought into the freedom and glory of the children of God."[21] The nations rage and the One enthroned in heaven laughs.[22] *Do not be afraid. Take it in stride. Keep your emotional stability.*[23]

Concern number three: Apostasy. In the face of persecution, martyrdom, universal hatred and animosity, be prepared for the church to decline. "Many will turn away from the faith and will betray and hate each other." False teachers will deceive many and many believers will succumb to wickedness and "the love of most will grow cold, but whoever (singular) stands firm to the end will be saved." The alternative to falling away is the Sermon on the Mount revisited and living the Jesus' way. Real disciples show love instead of hate, practice purity instead of lust, seek reconciliation, not retaliation, and stand firm to the end. In the face of apostasy, church decline, and hate, missions explodes! "And this gospel of the kingdom will be preached in the whole world as a testimony to all nations, and then the end

---

21. Romans 8:20-21.
22. Psalm 2:1-4.
23. Bruner, p. 482.

will come." The bottom line is this: *Do not give up. Preach the gospel of the kingdom. Keep the Faith.*

These three concerns: deception, fear and apostasy, are overcome by discernment, love, and faithfulness. This motley minority of real Christians, hated by the world and even by *many* professing and "successful" Christians, will *successfully* preach the gospel of the kingdom to the world as a testimony to all nations. According to Jesus, this is how it will be right up to the end. These are the on-going dynamics that the body of Christ will face in every generation.

The climax of the first movement of this apocalyptic symphony is the destruction of the temple. The first cycle of deception, fear and apostasy will end in AD 70 when Rome destroys the temple, but the cycle of deception, fear, and apostasy will be repeated over and over again. Jesus warns the first generation of disciples that the *end* of the *beginning-of-the-end* will be cataclysmic. Jesus draws on the language and themes of Daniel, Isaiah, and Zechariah to describe the destruction of the temple and its impact on the world-wide body of Christ.

The message for us is this: What the first generation of Jewish Christians faced is paradigmatic for future generations of disciples. The "great distress, unequaled from the beginning of the world until now—and never to be equaled again," becomes a theme throughout church history. Jesus warns believers that they will face false messiahs and false prophets, who perform great signs and wonders, but they must not fall for it. Don't be fooled. Don't be deceived. The coming of the Son of Man will be as obvious as lightning. Jesus warns believers of great social upheaval, but there is no reason to panic. God is in control. Jesus concludes this section with an apocalyptic description of the world-wide success of the mission of God:

"And he will send his angels [messengers] with a loud trumpet call, and they will gather his elect from the four winds, from one end of the heavens to the other."[24]

Understanding this does not require special insight or secret knowledge. It is as simple and straightforward as recognizing that Spring is coming in the green tender twigs of the fig tree. Anyone who implies otherwise is a false prophet leading people astray. In his Sermon on the End of the World, Jesus prepares not only the first disciples but the last disciples for his Coming. Jesus dampens speculation and ramps up readiness. His sermon calls for commitment, not curiosity; patient endurance, not complacency.

The fact that the first and the last generations of believers are in view is underscored by Jesus in three ways: (1) No one knows, not even the Son of Man, when the final end will come. Only the Father knows. (2) Noah's age is typical of the end of the age. Everything will go on as normal. People will be eating and drinking, marrying and giving in marriage right up to the end. (3) No one will be expecting the Lord's return when it comes. Everyone will be doing their regular work and in their normal routine. "People who seem so similar at work will be shown dramatically dissimilar at the Judgment."[25]

FEAR-OF-THE-LORD PARABOLIC

Jesus likens the coming of the Son of Man to a midnight break-in. The emotive element behind the metaphor is fear and the purpose of the metaphor is readiness. It may strike some believers as incongruous that Jesus would compare the glorious

---

24. Matthew 24:11.
25. Bruner, p. 527.

coming of the Son of Man to a burglary. Why not encourage readiness with a positive metaphor? Cheer people on with a can-do attitude, rather than play on their insecurities. But I doubt that Jesus would change his metaphor to suit our sensitivities. His mini-parable lays down the right emphasis. To make his point, he draws a parallel between home security and eternal security. We need to cultivate a healthy fear of what is expected of us. Jesus promised to never leave us nor forsake us. We can count on it, "All things work together for good to those who love God and are called according to his purpose."[26] But God's faithfulness is no excuse for our faithlessness. Jesus holds us accountable and challenges us to meet our vulnerabilities with vigilance. Stay alert.

The Word of God says, "The fear of the Lord is the beginning of wisdom." Biblical scholars tell us that this is a bound phrase. We miss the meaning of fear-of-the-Lord when we look up "fear" in the dictionary and then "God" and piece together a definition. Fear-of-the-Lord means living our lives in the presence of God moment by moment, with all the awe, obedience, humility, love and courage that such living requires. It is a common and comprehensive term for referring to the way we live the spiritual life. Eugene Peterson calls it "the stock biblical phrase for the way of life that is lived responsively and appropriately before who God is, who he is as Father, Son, and Holy Spirit."[27]

These three parables are fear-of-the-Lord parables for two reasons. First, because they teach us what the fear-of-the-Lord

---

26. Romans 8:28.

27. Eugene H. Peterson, *Christ Plays in Ten Thousand Places* (Grand Rapids, MI: Eerdmans, 2005), p. 41.

is. In Psalm 34, David prays, "Come, my children, listen to me; I will teach you the fear of the Lord." The fear-of-the-Lord is like no other fear. Earlier in the psalm, David praised God, saying, "I sought the Lord, and he answered me; he delivered me from all my fears."[28] In the same psalm, David contrasts "all my fears" with the fear-of-the-Lord. To be delivered from our fears is to embrace the fear-of-the-Lord. This is what John meant when he said, "perfect love drives out fear."[29] In the wilderness, Moses distinguished between being afraid and the fear-of-the-Lord. He said to the people, "Do not be afraid. God has come to test you, so that the fear of God will be with you to keep you from sinning."[30] In the early church, Luke reports that Barnabas helped Jerusalem Christians overcome their fear of Saul even as he describes them "living in the fear-of-the-Lord."[31] Second, because these three parables put the fear-of-the-Lord in us. Jesus was deadly earnest when he taught that the consequences of selfishness, thoughtlessness and uselessness are devastating. He made it clear that we could lose our soul over these matters.

Option number one: *fear-of-the-Lord faithfulness or selfish unfaithfulness.*

The master entrusts all his household servants to a faithful and wise servant "to give them their food at the proper time." "But suppose that servant is wicked and says to himself, 'My master is staying away for a long time,' and he then begins to beat up his fellow servants and to party all the time." If you are tracking with Jesus, you are asking yourself the significance of providing *food* at *the proper time* or *in season.* Jesus' admoni-

---

28. Psalm 34:4.
29. 1 John 4:18.
30. Exodus 20:20.
31. Acts 9:26, 31.

tion to Peter, "feed my sheep," comes to mind.[32] Gospel truth delivered in a timely fashion. "'The food' means revelation; 'in season' means relevance."[33] When the master returns and discovers that this servant has been playing master, that he has abused his power and has been harsh with the other servants, he is judged severely—very severely. "He will cut him to pieces and assign him a place with the hypocrites, where there will be weeping and gnashing of teeth."[34] Jesus isn't fooling around. Faithfulness until he returns, no matter how far off, is expected.

Option number two: *fear-of-the-Lord faithfulness or thoughtless unfaithfulness.*

Jesus likened the coming kingdom of heaven to a wedding ceremony with ten bridesmaids. The role of these girls in the ceremony may have been to escort the bridegroom in a torchlight procession.[35] Five of them were foolish and five were wise. Five silly girls compared to five sensible girls. The thoughtful bridesmaids are a picture of the long-obedience in the same direction. They have the reserved energy to go the distance. Their lamps will remain lit. They have the "oil" of disciplined, discipled faith in Christ. They are prepared for either a long delay or an immediate return of the bridegroom. The thoughtless bridesmaids on the other hand, are flighty and unprepared for the midnight entrance of the bridegroom. The foolish bridesmaids are a picture of shallow faith, maybe even excited and enthusiastic faith, but without depth and obedience. They represent distracted, overly dependent and irresponsibly weak

---

32. John 21:15-18.
33. Bruner, p. 538.
34. Matthew 24:51.
35. R. T. France, *The Gospel of Matthew: The New International Commentary* (Grand Rapids, MI: Eerdmans, 2007), p. 947.

believers, who may say, "Lord, Lord" and feel spiritual, but they are not. They are thoughtless and the Lord comes down hard on them. "Truly I tell you, I don't know you." In the first parable, the Lord comes sooner than expected; in the second parable, he comes later than expected. Jesus' bottom line: "So keep alert because you just don't know the day or the hour." Readiness cannot be achieved by "last minute adjustments," but depends on "long-term provision."[36]

Option number three: *fear-of-the-Lord faithfulness or fearful unfaithfulness.*

A very wealthy master entrusted his wealth to his three servants and left on a journey. This is like our Master, the Lord Jesus, who entrusts his wealth, the gospel, to the church in this interim period before he comes again. By most accounts, these three individuals were given a huge amount of capital to invest. If a single talent was worth six to ten thousand denarii, as some scholars have suggested, and a denarius was worth a fair day's wage, then the sum of money is vast — "the equivalent of approximately a whole lifetime of wages."[37] The amount of the investment gets our attention. It is hyperbolic. People like Warren Buffett or Bill Gates come to mind. The talent is whatever the Lord has given to us in the gospel and for the sake of the gospel. Talent has mission written all over it. Talent means the opportunity to live and preach the gospel of grace.

The parable sets up a comparison between the two servants who invest what they have received and the third who buries his talent. *Receiving* underscores the grace that precedes the work, followed by three aggressive action verbs that emphasize

36. France, p. 947.
37. Bruner, p. 553.

the effort. Two servants immediately *moved out, went to work,* and *won* more money. The third servant went off, "dug a hole in the ground and hid his master's money." Instead of moving out, he retreated, instead of going to work, he dug a hole, and instead of winning more, he hid what he had. When the master returned to settle accounts the two servants are commended for gaining a profit. The servant who had received five talents was proud of his success: "Master, *you* entrusted me with five bags of gold. See, *I* have gained five more." He's brimming with confidence and joy. "Here is a joy in work that should not be depressed by a heavy-handed spirituality. Jesus wants disciples to feel good about their work."[38]

Both servants receive identical words of praise: "Well done, good and faithful servant! You have been faithful with a few things; I will put you in charge of many things. Come and share your master's happiness!" "Human beings have been created to be goal-and-praise-oriented. The single great goal of Christians can be to hear their Lord's 'Wonderful!' spoken to their life work at the Judgment. We cannot live without laying up treasures *somewhere* — so we can lay them up in heaven. . ."[39] The two servants used the first person personal pronoun *"I"* as it should be used, a confident, well-earned declaration. They share the right kind of pride in the Master's work and they seek the Master's reward.

The negative force of the parable of the talents falls on the third servant who squanders the opportunity to invest his master's talent. He blamed the master for this: "Master," he said, "I knew that you are a hard man (*sklēros*), harvesting

---

38. Bruner, p. 557.
39. Bruner, p. 557.

where you have not sown and gathering where you have not scattered seed. So I was afraid and went out and hid your gold in the ground. See, here is what belongs to you." The freedom and joy of the first two servants to go quickly and invest everything testifies against the third servant's indictment against the master. They lived life unhindered. They took their whole investment and put it to work to please the master. How was the third servant able to conclude that the master was harsh and unreasonable, if not out of his own imagination? He imposed his own harsh standards on any investment strategy. He fell victim to his own conservatism. He projected himself onto the master. He responded to the opportunity as he would act if he were the master. He refused to acknowledge the investment as a trust. He saw it only as a liability. We can be thankful that the master is not anything like the harsh task-master envisioned by the third servant.

Many New Testament scholars liken the third servant to the Pharisees who labored under a false and self-imposed view of God's grace-less rigidity. The Pharisees were unwilling and unprepared to do anything with the gospel, but bury it under their self-righteous rules, regulations, and traditions. They succeeded in crucifying Jesus and *burying* him. The third servant's strategy recalls C. S. Lewis' image of the casket. "There is no safe investment. To love at all is to be vulnerable." *To really invest your life, your time, your energy, and your resources in Christ is to be vulnerable.* To live the Jesus way is risky business. If you want to keep your heart intact, if you want to play it safe, then you don't want to risk anything, much less your all. Lewis' advice for the bury-it-in-the-ground type servant is to protect your heart.

Wrap it carefully round with hobbies and little luxuries; avoid all entanglements; lock it safe in the casket or coffin of your selfishness.[40]

"Look, here's your money!" Did the third servant honestly think the master would be pleased? One gets the impression, "of a bad conscience wrapping itself in 'good' theology."[41] And in this case the so-called 'good' theology is heretical in the worst way, because it *sounds* right. But the third servant's theology is false. His bad theology is presumptuous, pretentious, and narcissistic. The third servant imposed his strong and twisted view on the master. Sacrilege can go up as well as down. Obsequious piety is offensive to God, ranking right up there with blasphemy. If he thought he was honoring the master by burying the master's money, he was mistaken. No matter how well-intentioned his risk free strategy was, he had diminished the investment and insulted the master. He had done nothing. It would have been better if he had never received the money in the first place.

The master exploded, "You wicked, lazy servant!" He issued orders, "Give his talent to the one who has ten and throw that worthless servant outside, into the darkness, where there will be weeping and gnashing of teeth." "This parable is unique," writes Bruner, "in attacking *humility*."[42] This is a false humility in every way. The humility that confidently knows where the gospel is buried, whether in creed or doctrine or tradition or sermon, but never embraces the gospel, never risks anything for the sake of

40. C.S. Lewis, *The Four Loves* (San Diego, CA: Harvest Book, 1960), p. 121.

41. Bruner, p. 561.

42. Bruner, p. 561.

the gospel. This is the humility that prides itself on grace, but knows nothing of the costly grace that demands one's all. The first two servants share in their master's happiness, but the self-preoccupied and self-pleasing third servant is cast out into utter darkness. Jesus' scary story hits home. The third servant in Jesus' parable of the talents was oblivious to his danger. He never saw the judgment coming. He was caught off-guard.

These are fear-of-the-Lord parables because the Lord is serious about our faithfulness. Professing believers who are selfishly, thoughtlessly, and fearfully unfaithful will face extreme consequences. Jesus isn't kidding. We can assent to a few ideas about Jesus and then go on about our life as if nothing has changed, but there's hell to pay. To believe is to obey and to obey is to believe. Jesus is clear about the consequences, if we don't believe and obey.

Unlike the selfish servant we are committed to the household of faith. "We proclaim *Christ*, admonishing and teaching everyone with all wisdom, so that we may present everyone fully mature in Christ. To this end *we* strenuously contend with all the energy Christ so powerfully works in *us*."[43] Unlike the silly bridesmaids we are committed to the long obedience in the same direction. "*We* are confident that he who began a good work in *us* will carry it on to completion until the day of Christ Jesus."[44] Unlike the useless servant we are committed to investing the gospel in every possible way. We want to put the gospel to work in everything we say and do. "I don't know about you," Paul urges, "but I'm running hard for the finish line. I'm giving it everything I've got. No sloppy living for me! I'm staying

---

43. Colossians 1:28-29.
44. Philippians 1:6.

alert and in top condition. I'm not going to get caught napping, telling everyone else all about it and then missing out myself."[45]

THE LAST JUDGMENT

Modern preachers end their sermons positively; Jesus ended decisively, with layers of metaphor and admonition communicating a single message—a call for decision and action. Jesus closed the Sermon on the Mount with mini-summaries, word pictures, visualizing truth and comprehending the message. Choose the narrow gate. Watch out for false prophets. Produce good fruit. Build your house on bedrock.

The Sermon on the End of the World concludes in similar fashion with a graphic picture of the Judgment. Once again, as in the Sermon on the Mount, it is an *either/or* situation. No in-between state. No middle ground. We are either in or out, accepted or rejected, blessed or cursed. Jesus' last sermon recalls Moses' last sermon. "Take to heart all the words I have solemnly declared to you this day..."[46] The Sermon on the End ends where it began by drawing attention to people in need and to the people who meet those needs. Jesus commended the poor widow for her sacrificial giving. The invisible people ignored and overlooked by the world become the center of attention. Jesus expects us to see those in need.

Jesus describes the process of separation in parabolic terms. It is like a shepherd separating the sheep from the goats. Two groups stand before the Son of Man when he comes in all his glory. He is the King and he will say to those on his right, "Come, you who are *blessed by my Father*; take your inheri-

---

45. 1 Corinthians 9:24-27, The Message.
46. Deuteronomy 32:46.

tance, the kingdom prepared for you since the creation of the world." We must not skip over these powerful truths. Those on the King's right are "blessed by my Father" and recipients of the inheritance prepared since the creation of the world.

The Reformers insisted that we are saved by faith alone, but saving faith is never alone. True faith in Christ is always accompanied by the works of Christ. We not only have faith *in* Jesus but we demonstrate the faith *of* Jesus. Beatitude-based living begins with grace but does not lack works. "Blessed are the merciful for they will be shown mercy." "Blessed are those who hunger and thirst after righteousness for they will be filled."

Those on the right are *not* commended for performing great signs and wonders. They are commended for feeding the hungry, giving water to the thirsty, hospitality to the stranger, clothes to the needy, care for the sick, and friendship to the imprisoned. Moreover they do this naturally, automatically, routinely. Need-meeting in the name of Jesus is who they are. It is no pious big deal. They follow Jesus and this is what disciples who are saved by grace through faith do with their lives. The Gospel of Jesus Christ plays itself out in 10,000 ways in the daily routine of ordinary self-less concern for the other. Life is marked by the principle of the cross. The description reminds us of Jesus' Who-Is-My-Neighbor parable.

There is something beautiful about the ignorance of those on the right: "Lord, when did we see you hungry and feed you, or thirsty and give you something to drink? When did we see you a stranger and invite you in, or needing clothes and clothe you? When did we see you sick or in prison and go and visit you?" This is an ignorance that runs contrary to the presumption of works righteousness. It fits with "so-that-no-one-can-boast" salvation by grace through faith. Because of Jesus Christ the righteous care for the needy and they do so without showy piety or inflated spirituality. This is a beautiful picture of the priesthood of all believers engaged in kingdom work. Everybody in Christ is involved in meeting real needs. The sermon begins with Jesus' disciples asking *when* will the temple will be destroyed and the sermon ends with Jesus' disciples (those on his right) asking *when* did we see you in need. We have moved from curiosity to compassion and from speculation to action. Instead of *when is the end?* the question is: *how then shall we live?*

This is a provocative picture for those who say they don't know where to minster. Jesus would say to us, *"Get a life. Mix it up. Put yourself in the company of the needy. Keep your eyes peeled for poor widows. Don't divert your eyes from the lame. Pay attention to them. Let's not make ministry into a mystery. Get in the game. Just do it!"*

Like the Pharisees who debated the identity of their neighbor, people have been known to debate who are the "least of these." Since when did being nice to Christians confirm that one is a Christian? Didn't Jesus say, "Love your enemies and pray for those who persecute you"? Didn't he condemn the Pharisees for loving only their own kind? Remember Jesus gave living water to the woman at the well. He gave the bread and the cup to Judas and he prayed with the thief on the cross. The least of these are the least of these and everyone is a potential brother or sister in Christ. James said it well: "Religion that God our Father accepts as pure and faultless is this: to look after orphans and widows in their distress and to keep oneself from being polluted by the world."[47] The holy naivete of those on the right is beautiful for its lack of self-preoccupation and preten-

---

47. James 1:27.

sion. In Christ, they follow the Jesus way and serve regardless of whether the person is deemed important or not in the eyes of the world. Christ's disciples can do no other.

The ignorance of those on the left, however, is inexcusable. Those on the right are "blessed by my Father" but those on the left only have themselves to blame for being cursed. Their disregard of needy people is consistent with their failure to follow Christ. What we do for others we do for Christ; what we don't do for others, we don't do for Christ. These people on the left are all talk. Big talkers. They are the super-Christians, who "perform great signs and wonders." They are like the wicked servant who beat up the household staff. They are like the five bridesmaids, unprepared for the coming of the bridegroom, who replies to their excuses, "Truly I tell you, I don't know you." They are like the worthless servant who blamed the master for his failure to invest. Whatever judgment those on the left deserve has been earned entirely on their own. The implication is that these are professing disciples. They speak to the Lord with a confident and familiar air. They are at home with church lingo. The conclusion of the sermon highlights the real problem in the church: people who claim big things for God, but in reality they come off acting like the Pharisees. Jesus seems intent on warning the disciples not to become like the Pharisees whom he had just condemned before leaving the temple.

EDGY CHRISTIANS

To be in the company of ordinary believers who are not all talk is a privilege. Edgy Christians practice the fear-of-the-Lord in daily living. By God's grace, they meet the needs of others in the name of Jesus and in Christ's love. Like the poor widow commended by Jesus as he was leaving the temple, they do not draw attention to their sacrificial love, but they see the needs of God's invisible children and adults. They confront life's challenges with a growing dependence upon the Lord. They face grave illnesses without bitterness and self-centeredness and with firm resolve they worship the Lord and minister to others. They live on the radical edge of living for God. Jesus is Lord.

The parents of a psychologically ill son never dreamed they would have to walk through this dark night of the soul. The frustration of it all would be enough to put many over the edge, but as his father Ben explained, it is the meaningfulness of Christ's gift of salvation that inspires him. One night he was coming home from church and listening to a CD of worship music. Suddenly he was overwhelmed by the truth of the Incarnation. He was so moved he couldn't stop crying, not out of self-pity or anger, but out of a sense of God's deep love and joy. Jesus is Lord.

I marvel at the irrepressible joy of Judy. She is married to Brian who is HIV positive. Her husband has hemophilia and contracted the virus through a tainted blood transfusion. It would be enough for Judy to focus on her husband, which she does with wonderful energy and happiness, but she has a heart for the poor and destitute in Liberia. She pours herself into caring for the poor with enthusiasm and wisdom. Another woman in her situation might lament her husband's health and feel sorry for herself, but not Judy. Her husband's needs and the needs of others, even those of the poor in Liberia, move her ever closer to her Savior. Jesus is Lord.

A close friend who has weathered intense suffering with great perseverance and witness, said to me, "I wouldn't share this with most people, but I feel like a Bible character." His instincts were right. As we live lives marked by the cross in daily dependence upon the grace of Christ, we identify with those lead characters in salvation history. We become like them and they become like us. We are one. As they were called, we are called. Jesus is Lord.

The Sermon on the End of the World is a message for disciples. It is designed to get us ready. Jesus calls for discernment, resilience, readiness, obedience, and ministry in his name. Don't be deceived, distracted, or confused. Don't become fearful, complacent, lazy, or indifferent to the needs around you. Jesus' message has two themes woven together: no-fear-apocalyptic and fear-of-the-Lord parabolic. Wake up. Keep watch. Stay alert. Be prepared. Invest in God's kingdom work. Make the most of your ministry opportunities! Amen. Jesus is Lord.

8

TEXT TO TABLE

Every sermon should move from the pulpit to the table smoothly. For all that has been said about tension, the transition from text to table ought to be free of tension. The pattern in this tapestry of truth that we preach and teach reveals the crucified Lord Jesus. Preaching weaves together proclamation and the eucharistic celebration.

On the road to Emmaus, Jesus told the story of salvation history. In seven miles, he drew out its salvation-making, history-changing, life-transforming significance. The two disciples felt the impact of the Word of God rightly divided: "Were not our hearts burning within us while he talked with us on the road and opened the Scriptures to us?" This is what good preaching accomplishes.

When they reached Emmaus, Jesus made it seem as if he were going to continue on. Jesus neither presumed on their receptivity nor imposed his will. On the way, Jesus embodied the humility true of all good preaching. He pursued them as a stranger. He entered into dialogue with them. He ignored their wrong perception of him. He solicited their perspective and he waited for their invitation. The preacher's ego is sublimated to the gospel text. The two disciples "urged him strongly, 'Stay with us . . . '" The implication is that Jesus' teaching was so compelling that they did not want him to stop. They invited Jesus into their home.

Luke makes us aware of the tension in the text. There is a tension between context and content. The setting stands in contrast to the significance of the message. The ordinary setting becomes the occasion for extraordinary truth. All the work we study in seminary, including evangelism, theology, biblical exegesis, spiritual formation and preaching ought to be worked into daily life. Everything worth teaching and learning is translated into a dialogue along the way. The best place for this truth is not in the rarefied atmosphere of the academy or within the hallowed walls of the cathedral. It was meant to be discussed along the way.

Spirituality is often squeezed into a corner of life reserved for pious reflections and church services. But God intended spirituality to be at the center of our ordinary, everyday life together. The apostle Paul's challenge remains, *"So here's what I want you to do, God helping you: Take your everyday, ordinary life—your sleeping, eating, going-to-work, and walking around life—and place it before God as an offering."*[1]

The journey from Jerusalem to table fellowship in Emmaus is reminiscent of the pedagogical scene described in Deuteronomy 6. The "classroom" is daily life. "Talk about them when you sit at home and when you walk along the road, when you lie down and when you get up."

---

1.   Romans 12:1, *The Message*

On the Emmaus road there was a tension between belief and unbelief. The risen Lord was perceived as an ignorant stranger. The practical purpose of the disciples' delayed recognition was to give them the opportunity to absorb the message intellectually. They met the risen Lord by grasping the truth of the Savior. Their eyes were opened and they recognized him, because the Lord opened the Scriptures for them. The moment of personal recognition came at the table, when Jesus took bread, gave thanks, broke it and began to give it to them. In that Eucharistic moment, they discovered the Person of Christ because they understood the Work of Christ. But for all this tension between identification and recognition, there was no tension between text and table!

The table is the altar call for the preached text. The Word proclaimed is the Word remembered, internalized, and eaten as food for the soul. The words of institution, "This is my body broken for you," and "This cup is the new covenant that I pour out with my blood," signify the whole body of revealed truth. They include the whole counsel of God from Genesis to Revelation. The sermon ends with four simple action verbs: take, thank, break, and give. As we partake of the bread and the cup we participate in Christ receiving, thanking, sacrificing, and giving. The mission of God begins and ends at this table in fellowship with the crucified and risen Lord Jesus Christ. A good question for the preacher to ask is this: did Jesus have to die to preach this sermon? If the preacher moves from the sermon to the sacrifice awkwardly or concludes the sermon as if Holy Communion is an entirely different matter, then chances are Jesus did not have to die to preach that sermon. It may have been a moralistic sermon or an entertaining sermon or an uplifting sermon, but it wasn't an evangelistic sermon—even though it may have called people forward to accept Jesus. All evangelistic sermons are eucharistic sermons. Good sermons bring us to the table of the Lord.

Table fellowship works into the New Testament narrative so unobtrusively that we can almost miss it. Sharing a simple meal provided the context for much of Jesus' interaction with his disciples. I doubt that it was coincidental that Jesus designed spiritual growth around meal time. In his ministry, physical and spiritual nourishment ran together in the ordinary course of daily life. Jesus' *modus operandi* involved the whole person. He fed the body and the soul. Jesus broke bread with the disciples before instituting the Lord's Supper and before praying for them. He fixed breakfast for Peter before leading Peter to reconciliation. After the resurrection, but before the Ascension, Luke describes the setting this way: "On one occasion, while he was *eating* with them, he gave this command . . . "[2] Jesus promised the Holy Spirit over dinner with the disciples. The ambience must not have been super-spiritual, no incense or prepared liturgy, just a simple meal. The Jesus way of relating to people rules out any method or manner that is artificially contrived or self-consciously "spiritual." Jesus is real and he models the way he expects us to relate to one another. We need to pay attention.

The Table of the Lord is the ultimate family meal and it is hosted by the Lord himself. Jesus brings the message home around the kitchen table. A good friend would encourage me after a Sunday sermon saying, "You really brought it home today." The preacher moves from the text to the table, bringing the Word home, so we can metabolize it into every fiber of our being.

---

2.   Acts 1:4

LaVergne, TN USA
28 April 2010
180586LV00006B/1/P